Linguistic Expressions and Semantic Processing

Alastair Butler

Linguistic Expressions and Semantic Processing

A Practical Approach

 Springer

Alastair Butler
Center for the Advancement
  of Higher Education
Tohoku University
Sendai
Japan

ISBN 978-3-319-38610-2   ISBN 978-3-319-18830-0   (eBook)
DOI 10.1007/978-3-319-18830-0

Springer Cham Heidelberg New York Dordrecht London

Printed on acid-free paper

Springer International Publishing AG Switzerland is part of Springer Science+Business Media
(www.springer.com)

Preface

This book develops ways of processing linguistic expressions to return what can be described as *meanings*. The linguistic expressions are from a series of related formal languages that capture properties of natural language in a controlled and systematic fashion. They also offer a wide perspective on natural language that is cross-linguistic by nature. While examples are related to the English language, applicability is expected to carry over to other natural languages, unless explicitly noted otherwise.

Much of this book involves presenting formal machinery and then working through consequences. Motivation is found with finding methods that are flexible but constrained to support processing structures close to expected conventional parsings of natural language. To help, computer programs are used to provide "hands on" experience. In fact, the formal definitions are already executable computer programs of the programming language Standard ML.

Having its origins as a meta-language for defining proof tactics in interactive theorem provers, Standard ML provides an excellent choice for implementing linguistic theories. Standard ML is a (mostly) functional language and so provides notation and concepts that are similar to those of mathematics, so much so that the programs of this book are written in a manner nearly identical to the formal mathematical spelling out of the theory, only with the advantage of being quite literally brought to life. While written for clarity rather than efficiency, the programs cope well with large-sized examples. Their simplicity makes them an ideal vehicle for further developments, and the reader is encouraged to experiment with them. They are available on the Internet at http://www.compling.jp.

The book is structured as follows:

Chapter 1 introduces predicate languages that are the basis for the formalization of linguistic expressions considered in this book. Preparing the ground for the rest of the book, this chapter defines syntactic trees enriched with the concepts of binding and scope, as well as some associated routines for gathering information, pretty-printing, and post-processing. The chapter also introduces the model theoretic semantics of first-order predicate logic, presenting models, assignments, and a Tarskian satisfaction relation.

The remaining chapters focus on developing the evaluation techniques that underlie the definition of satisfaction, only with limitation to the aim of realizing mechanisms for returning predicate language expressions as representations of meanings derived by evaluation from inputs that are ultimately conventional phrase structure parsings of natural language.

Specifically, Chap. 2 adds an If conditional to a recursive routine for evaluating expressions against an assignment function that stores accumulated binding information. Assignments are considered that assign sequences as values, so what is evaluated can be selected based on tests regarding lengths of assigned sequences. This allows for a robust interpretation of unknown lexical items and for feeding an automated regulation of binding information to leave little need for explicitly coding dependencies.

Chapter 3 develops utilizing the assignment as a source of information about the content of the expression under evaluation, with assignments governing where dependencies are located throughout an evaluation. This is achieved with a language that includes fine grained and often interdependent primitive operations of scope manipulation to support processing structures close to expected conventional parsings of natural language.

Chapter 4 describes and illustrates treebank annotation that with modest conversion serves as a syntactic base for feeding the evaluation mechanism of Chap. 3. This achieves a very broad coverage, with examples of passives, adverbial clauses, participial clauses, adjectives, adverbs, floating quantifiers, pronominal binding, covaluation arising because of embedding, wh-questions, relative clauses, free relative clauses, comparative clauses, tough movement complements, clause-adjoined relative clauses, phrasal conjunction, speech parentheticals, and nouns of address.

For readers not familiar with Standard ML, a concise summary of the core of the language is provided as an appendix.

This book emerged as output from a project under the Japan Science and Technology Agency (JST) PRESTO Sakigake program in the research area *Synthesis of Knowledge for Information Oriented Society* (2010–2014). Being part of this was an incredible experience and privilege. I thank Hideyuki Nakashima and Hideki Asou and other advisors for their support, supervision, and encouragement. While writing this book I received help and motivation from many people, including Daisuke Bekki, Yasuko Butler, Tsaiwei Fang, Shota Hiyama, Natsuha Katakura, Tomoya Kosuge, Loh Boon Liang, Pascual Martinez-Gomez, Koji Mineshima, Masaaki Nagata, Chidori Nakamura, Prashant Pardeshi, Takumi Toda, and Zhen Zhou, as well as the insightful comments of two anonymous reviewers, all of which I gratefully acknowledge. I also thank Federica Corradi Dell'Acqua for her guiding editorship. I am hugely indebted to Paul Dekker whose clarity of mechanism and vision I dare to hope rubbed off into this work. And most of all I thank Kei Yoshimoto, as collaborator on overlapping work, and the force of optimism and opportunity carrying this work to completion.

Sendai   Alastair Butler
January 2015

Contents

1 Predicate Languages.. 1
   1.1   Predicate Language Expressions 1
         1.1.1   Constructing Expressions......................... 2
         1.1.2   Scope, Binding, Being Free and Sentences......... 3
         1.1.3   Barendregt Variable Convention 5
         1.1.4   First-Order Predicate Logic Language 7
   1.2   First Order Predicate Logic Semantics..................... 9
         1.2.1   Models 9
         1.2.2   The Semantics 11
         1.2.3   Truth Definition 15
   1.3   A Target Language..................................... 16
         1.3.1   Post-processing............................ 17
         1.3.2   Davidsonian Representations 20
   1.4   Summary.. 24
   References... 24

2 Self-Selective Evaluation 25
   2.1   Sequence Assignments 26
   2.2   Self Language 28
   2.3   Applying the Self Language............................ 34
         2.3.1   Core Arguments 34
         2.3.2   Nouns and Noun Phrases...................... 38
         2.3.3   Adding Non Core Arguments................... 41
   2.4   Summary.. 44
   References... 44

3 Self-Locating Evaluation 45
   3.1   Scope Control Theory 45
   3.2   Evaluation 50

	3.3	Grammatical Roles, Arguments and Predicates	56
	3.3.1	Classic Arguments	57
	3.3.2	Predicates	58
	3.3.3	Noun Phrases	61
	3.3.4	Closures and (in)definites	62
	3.3.5	Proper Names	68
	3.3.6	Pronouns	70
	3.3.7	Quantification	73
	3.3.8	Verbs with Clause Embedding	75
	3.3.9	Control Embedding	78
	3.3.10	Nouns with Embedding	82
	3.4	Summary	84
	References		84

4 Treebank Annotation 85
	4.1	General Parsing Principles	86
	4.2	Clause Level Scope Annotation	90
	4.3	Conversion	91
	4.4	Passives	96
	4.5	Adverbial Clauses (CP-ADV)	99
	4.6	Participial Clauses (IP-PPL)	107
	4.7	Adjectives	113
	4.8	Adverbs	118
	4.9	Floating Quantifiers	121
	4.10	Pronominal Binding and Covaluation	123
	4.11	Binding and Covaluation with Quantification	128
	4.12	Wh-Questions (CP-QUE)	130
	4.13	Relative Clauses (CP-REL)	135
	4.14	Free Relative Clauses (CP-FRL)	138
	4.15	Comparative Clauses (CP-CMP)	140
	4.16	Tough Movement Complements (CP-TMC)	142
	4.17	Clause-Adjoined Relative Clauses (CP-CAR)	144
	4.18	Phrasal Conjunction (CONJP)	146
	4.19	Parentheticals	153
	4.20	Speech Parentheticals (IP-MAT-PRN)	155
	4.21	Nouns of Address	157
	4.22	Summary	159
	References		160

Appendix A: Standard ML Introduction 161

Index 171

Chapter 1
Predicate Languages

From the standpoint pursued in this book, the purpose of a linguistic expression is to provide guidance that makes semantic processing possible, with semantic processing culminating in what can be described as a *meaning*. As something concrete that might be spoken or written, a linguistic expression can be captured with strings of characters from some alphabet. But such surface renderings offer little structure to process.

More in the way of a handle is achieved by considering how linguistic expressions are composed of phrases (noun phrases, preposition phrases, clauses, and so forth). With such syntactic analysis, linguistic expressions are trees, or *parsed expressions*, whose nodes are labels that can be word level part-of-speech tags (N, P, ADJ, etc.), or phrase level categories (NP, PP, ADJP, etc.). Such parsed expressions are met in Chap. 4 and are shown to provide information to support considerable semantic processing. But with this opening chapter much more explicit structure is necessary, namely, syntax trees that are enriched with the concepts of binding and scope.

Section 1.1 introduces expressions of a particular kind of formal language with binding and scope called a *predicate language*, further narrowing attention to the language of *first-order predicate logic* with a pretty printing procedure. Section 1.2 introduces a model-theoretic semantics for the language of first-order predicate logic. Section 1.3 defines a general predicate language that will serve as a target language for meaning representations in the remainder of this book. Section 1.4 provides a summary.

1.1 Predicate Language Expressions

In this section the purpose of predicate languages is pushed aside to concentrate instead on specifying what a predicate language is in syntactic terms. Section 1.1.1 introduces predicate language expressions with a Standard ML (Milner et al. 1997) datatype. Section 1.1.2 looks at notions of scope, binding, being free and sentence. Section 1.1.3 considers motivation for obeying the Barendregt variable convention.

© Springer International Publishing Switzerland 2015
A. Butler, *Linguistic Expressions and Semantic Processing*,
DOI 10.1007/978-3-319-18830-0_1

Section 1.1.4 limits expressions to the language of first-order predicate logic with a pretty printing procedure.

1.1.1 Constructing Expressions

Expressions of a predicate language can be implemented in Standard ML as constructed values. Datatypes allow for novel ways to construct values from existing values. The datatype `Basic.t` defines a language that includes constructors to differentiate terms (`Basic.C` and `Basic.X`), code relations (`Basic.REL`) and build quantificational bindings (`Basic.QUANT`).

```
structure Basic =
struct

datatype t =
   C of string
 | X of int
 | REL of string * t list
 | QUANT of string * t list * t

end
```

This datatype is immediately useful both as a way of presenting predicate language expressions as well as a means for checking the validity of a given form. The following interactions with the Standard ML interactive prompt illustrate how errors in form are detected.

```
> Basic.QUANT ("∃", [Basic.X 1], Basic.REL ("boy", [Basic.X 1]));
```
val it =
QUANT ("∃", [X 1], REL ("boy", [X 1]))
: Basic.t

```
> Basic.QUAN ("∃", [Basic.X 1], Basic.REL ("boy", [Basic.X 1]));
```
Error-Value or constructor (QUAN) has not been declared in structure Basic
Found near Basic.QUAN ("∃", [Basic.X 1], Basic.REL (...))
Static Errors

```
> Basic.QUANT
     ("∃", [Basic.X 1], Basic.X 1, Basic.REL ("boy", [Basic.X 1]));
```
Error-Type error in function application.
  *Function: Basic.QUANT : string * Basic.t list * Basic.t -> Basic.t*
  Argument: ("∃", [Basic.X 1], Basic.X 1, Basic.REL (...)) :
    *string * Basic.t list * Basic.t * Basic.t*
  Reason:
    *Can't unify string * Basic.t list * Basic.t to*

*string * Basic.t list * Basic.t * Basic.t (Different number of fields)*
Found near Basic.QUANT ("∃", [Basic.X 1], Basic.X 1, ...)
Static Errors

For an example of using the `Basic.t` datatype, consider `allSubeprs`. This takes a predicate language expression `f` and returns a list of all the subexpressions of `f`, where the subexpressions of an expression `f` are `f` itself and all the expressions used to build `f`. Such a routine illustrates a simple instance of syntactic analysis.

```
fun allSubeprs (f: Basic.t): Basic.t list =
 case f of
   Basic.REL (s, es) =>
     [Basic.REL (s, es)] @ List.concat (map allSubeprs es)
 | Basic.QUANT (s, xs, e) =>
     [Basic.QUANT (s, xs, e)] @ allSubeprs e
 | _ => nil
```

It is now possible to provide a list of all the subexpressions of an expression, say `ex1`:

```
val ex1 =
Basic.REL ("¬", [
 Basic.QUANT ("∃", [Basic.X 1],
   Basic.REL ("∧", [
    Basic.REL ("boy", [Basic.X 1]),
    Basic.REL ("see", [Basic.C "yasuko", Basic.X 1])])])])
```

> `allSubeprs ex1;`
val it =
[REL ("¬", [
QUANT ("∃", [X 1],
REL ("∧", [REL ("boy", [X 1]), REL ("see", [C "yasuko", X 1])])])]),
QUANT ("∃", [X 1],
REL ("∧", [REL ("boy", [X 1]), REL ("see", [C "yasuko", X 1])])),
REL ("∧", [REL ("boy", [X 1]), REL ("see", [C "yasuko", X 1])]),
REL ("boy", [X 1]),
REL ("see", [C "yasuko", X 1])]
: Basic.t list

1.1.2 Scope, Binding, Being Free and Sentences

This section introduces the notions of scope, binding, being free and sentence. Scope for a quantifier can be defined in terms of (sub)expression structure, that is, in purely syntactic terms.

- Let e2 and Basic.QUANT (_, _, e3) be subexpressions of e1. e2 is said to occur in the **scope** of Basic.QUANT (_, _, e3) in e1 iff e2 occurs as a subexpression of e3.

The notion of scope offers the ability to capture portions of an expression. Binding as a notion refers to the region of smallest scope to give exact cases where variables are to be interpreted in the same way (as denoting the same object in the model; see Sect. 1.2.2).

- Basic.QUANT (_, [... x ...], e3) **binds** a variable x iff it is the quantifier with smallest scope containing x.

The following Standard ML routine, isBound, returns a list of all variables of an expression that are bound:

```
fun isBound (f: Basic.t): Basic.t list =
 case f of
   Basic.REL (_, es) => uniq (List.concat (map isBound es))
 | Basic.QUANT (_, xs, e) => uniq (xs @ isBound e)
 | _ => nil
```

Next the notion of being free is introduced:

- If an occurrence of a variable x is not bound, then the occurrence of x is said to be **free**.

The routine isFree takes an expression, f, and returns a list of all the free variables in f, that is, those variables that are not bound before being reached inside of f.

```
fun isFree (f: Basic.t): Basic.t list =
 case f of
   Basic.X i => [Basic.X i]
 | Basic.REL (_, es) => uniq (List.concat (map isFree es))
 | Basic.QUANT (_, xs, e) => diff (isFree e, xs)
 | _ => nil
```

Once there is the notion of being free, the notion of sentence can be defined:

- If an expression contains no occurrences of free variables then it is called a **sentence**.

isSentence will take an expression f and return true if f is a sentence (that is, an expression with no free variables), and false otherwise.

```
fun isSentence (f: Basic.t): bool =
 null (isFree f)
```

With an application of map, a list of quadruples for an expression can now be returned for all subexpressions of an expression, with each quadruple made up of an answer to whether the subexpression is a sentence, the list of bound variables, the list of free variables, and the subexpression itself. This can be demonstrated with ex1 of Sect. 1.1.1:

```
> map (fn e => (isSentence e, isBound e, isFree e, e))
    (allSubeprs ex1);
val it =
[(true, [X 1], [],
  REL ("¬", [
  QUANT ("∃", [X 1],
  REL ("∧", [REL ("boy", [X 1]), REL ("see", [C "yasuko", X 1])])])])),
(true, [X 1], [],
  QUANT ("∃", [X 1],
  REL ("∧", [REL ("boy", [X 1]), REL ("see", [C "yasuko", X 1])]))),
(false, [], [X 1],
  REL ("∧", [REL ("boy", [X 1]), REL ("see", [C "yasuko", X 1])])),
(false, [], [X 1], REL ("boy", [X 1])),
(false, [], [X 1], REL ("see", [C "yasuko", X 1]))]
: (bool * Basic.t list * Basic.t list * Basic.t) list
```

1.1.3 Barendregt Variable Convention

When constructing predicate language expressions care is required to ensure that variables are used appropriately. For example, consider the following Basic.t expression with its distinct variables Basic.X 1 and Basic.X 2:

```
Basic.QUANT ("∃", [Basic.X 1],
  Basic.QUANT ("∃", [Basic.X 2],
  Basic.REL ("∧", [
  e1,
  Basic.QUANT ("∃", [Basic.X 1], e2)])))
```

Assume the subexpressions e1 and e2 are expressions of arbitrary complexity that contain Basic.X 1 and Basic.X 2 free. Then each free occurrence of Basic.X 1 in e2 is bound by the inner Basic.QUANT ("∃", [Basic.X 1], _), and not the outer Basic.QUANT ("∃", [Basic.X 1], _). From the viewpoint of the outer Basic.QUANT ("∃", [Basic.X 1], _) this is an instance of *accidental hiding*: there can be no binding into e2 because of the occluding inner Basic.QUANT ("∃", [Basic.X 1], _). From the viewpoint of a free occurrence of Basic.X 1 inside e2 this is an occurrence of *accidental capture*: there is no way to form a dependency with the outer Basic.QUANT ("∃", [Basic.X 1], _), in contrast to Basic.QUANT ("∃", [Basic.X 2], _) which does bind into e2. Thus while the free occurrences of Basic.X 2 inside e1 and e2 are to be interpreted in the same way, this is not true for the free occurrences of Basic.X 1 inside e1 and e2.

To ensure that problems of accidental hiding and capture are avoided it is wise to keep to a general condition that all bound variables have names different from each other and from any free variables that may be used. This convention that free and bound names should always be kept disjoint and distinct from each other is often known as the 'Barendregt variable convention', following application of the convention to the lambda calculus in Barendregt (1984).

For a method to check whether an expression obeys the Barendregt convention, first a routine is defined to return a list of the variables that are re-used with quantification:

```
fun isReused (1: Basic.t list, f: Basic.t): Basic.t list =
 case f of
   Basic.REL (_, es) =>
   uniq (List.concat (map (fn e => isReused (1, e)) es))
 | Basic.QUANT (_, xs, e) =>
   List.filter (fn x => member (x, 1)) xs @ isReused (xs @ 1, e)
 | _ => nil
```

varConv checks of an expression f that there is no variable reuse with isReused (nil, f) and that there is no overlap between the contents of isBound f and isFree f.

```
fun varConv (f: Basic.t): bool =
 null (isReused (nil, f)) andalso
  null (List.filter (fn x => member(x, isBound f)) (isFree f))
```

The following application of map returns a list of quintuples for all subexpressions of an expression, with each quintuple made up of an answer from varConv as to whether the variable convention obtains, the list of reused variables, the list of bound variables, the list of free variables, and the subexpression itself.

```
val ex2 =
Basic.QUANT ("∃", [Basic.X 1],
 Basic.QUANT ("∃", [Basic.X 2],
  Basic.REL ("∧", [
   Basic.REL ("P", [Basic.X 1, Basic.X 2]),
   Basic.QUANT ("∃", [Basic.X 1],
    Basic.REL ("Q", [Basic.X 1, Basic.X 2]))])))

> map (fn e => (varConv e, isReused (nil, e), isBound e,
   isFree e, e)) (allSubeprs ex2);
val it =
[(false, [X 1], [X 1, X 2], [],
  QUANT ("∃", [X 1],
  QUANT ("∃", [X 2],
   REL ("∧", [REL ("P", [X 1, X 2]),
   QUANT ("∃", [X 1], REL ("Q", [X 1, X 2]))])))),
```

(false, [], [X 2, X 1], [X 1],
 QUANT ("∃", [X 2],
  REL ("∧", [REL ("P", [X 1, X 2]),
   QUANT ("∃", [X 1], REL ("Q", [X 1, X 2]))])))),
(false, [], [X 1], [X 1, X 2],
 REL ("∧", [REL ("P", [X 1, X 2]),
  QUANT ("∃", [X 1], REL ("Q", [X 1, X 2]))])))),
(true, [], [], [X 1, X 2], REL ("P", [X 1, X 2])),
(true, [], [X 1], [X 2], QUANT ("∃", [X 1], REL ("Q", [X 1, X 2])))),
(true, [], [], [X 1, X 2], REL ("Q", [X 1, X 2]))]
*: (bool * Basic.t list * Basic.t list * Basic.t list * Basic.t) list*

1.1.4 First-Order Predicate Logic Language

In this section the language of first-order predicate logic is defined. Atomic expressions are built as follows:

- If P is an n-place predicate and $x_1, \ldots x_n$ are either object constants or object variables, then $P(x_1, \ldots x_n)$ is an atomic expression.

To create more complicated assertions compound expressions are required. These are expressions built from atomic expressions by using a fixed set of propositional connectives and quantifiers. The following are the standard connectives of first-order predicate logic:

- $\exists x$ (existential quantifier, $\exists x B$ means "there is an x such that B").
- $\forall x$ (universal quantifier, $\forall x B$ means "for all x such that B").
- $\neg$ (negation symbol, $\neg B$ means "not B").
- $\rightarrow$ (implication symbol, $B \rightarrow C$ means "if B then C").
- $\wedge$ (conjunction symbol, $B \wedge C$ means "B and C").
- $\vee$ (disjunction symbol, $B \vee C$ means "B or C").

Having atomic expressions and connectives, the notion of expression for the first-order predicate logic language can be defined as follows:

1. Atomic expressions are expressions.
2. If B is an expression, and x is a variable, then $(\exists x B)$ and $(\forall x B)$ are also expressions.
3. If B and C are expressions, then $(\neg B)$, $(B \rightarrow C)$, $(B \wedge C)$ and $(B \vee C)$ are also expressions.

The `Basic.t` datatype can be used to build first-order predicate logic expressions. The following routine, `PrettyFol.eval`, converts a `Basic.t` expression that is an expression of first-order predicate logic into to a typeset string:

```
exception Error of string

structure PrettyFol =
struct

fun eval (f: Basic.t): string =
 let
  fun connect (s, es) =
   "(" ^ foldl (fn (b, a) => a ^ s ^ b) (hd es) (tl es) ^ ")"
 in
  case f of
    Basic.REL ("∧", es) =>
     connect (" ∧ ",  map eval es)
  | Basic.REL ("∨", es) =>
     connect (" ∨ ",  map eval es)
  | Basic.REL ("→", [e1, e2]) =>
     connect (" → ", map eval [e1, e2])
  | Basic.REL ("¬", [e]) => "¬"  ^ eval e
  | Basic.REL (s, es) =>
     s ^ connect (", ",
       map (fn Basic.C s => s
               | Basic.X i => "x" ^ Int.toString i
               | _ => raise (Error "invalid term")) es)
  | Basic.QUANT ("∀", [x], e) =>
     "∀" ^
       (fn Basic.X i => "x" ^ Int.toString i
          | _ => raise (Error "invalid term")) x ^ " " ^ eval e
  | Basic.QUANT ("∃", [x], e) =>
     "∃" ^
       (fn Basic.X i => "x" ^ Int.toString i
          | _ => raise (Error "invalid term")) x ^ " " ^ eval e
  | _ => raise (Error "invalid expression")
 end

end
```

For example, `ex1` of Sect. 1.1.1 can be pretty printed thus:

```
> PrettyFol.eval ex1;
```
val it = "¬ ∃x1 (boy(x1) ∧ see(yasuko, x1))": string

1.2 First Order Predicate Logic Semantics

So far predicate languages have provided expressions with binding and scope to represent meanings, but no way to realise meanings. This section introduces techniques of model-theoretic semantics to actualise meanings for the language of first order predicate logic by providing a means to calculate truth values. Section 1.2.1 describes first-order models. Section 1.2.2 presents a first-order model checker (or semantic evaluator), also introducing the key technical idea of an assignment function. The model checker takes a first-order model, an assignment function and a first-order expression as input and on this basis establishes whether the expression is satisfied (*true*) in the model with respect to the assignment function. Section 1.2.3 defines the notion of *truth*.

1.2.1 Models

Intuitively a model *is* a situation. For example, the picture below depicts the situation of a boy, namely Ren, on a hill with a tree flying a kite, and another boy, namely William, also on the hill, waving. There is also Yasuko, who is a girl with a dog, namely Rexx, and waving.

More formally, a model for a given vocabulary gives two pieces of information:

- First, the collection of entities that are in the situation; this collection, D, is usually called the *domain*.
- Second, for each symbol in the vocabulary of the predicate language under consideration, a *semantic entity* is given that is built from the items in D. This task is carried out by a function I called an *interpretation function*.

In set theoretic terms, a model M is an ordered pair (D, I) consisting of a domain D and an interpretation function I specifying semantic values over D.

A vocabulary will give a collection of n-place relation symbols and individual constant symbols. For example, consider the following vocabulary:

(1) arity 1 symbols: `"boy"`, `"girl"`, `"person"`, `"dog"`, `"hill"`, `"tree"`,
    `"kite"`, `"waves"`.
    arity 2 symbols: `"is_namely"`, `"is_boy_on"`, `"is_girl_with"`,
    `"is_hill_with"`, `"flies"`, `"sees"`.
    individual constant symbols: `"ren"`, `"william"`, `"yasuko"`, `"rexx"`.

Every symbol in the vocabulary needs to correspond to a semantic value. Arity n symbols are intended to denote n-place relations. In a model, each n-place relation symbol R should be interpreted as an n-place relation on D. That is, $I(R)$ should be a set of n-tuples of elements of D. More specifically:

- arity 1 symbols pick out subsets of D (that is, properties, or 1-place relations on D).
- arity 2 symbols pick out a 2-place relation on D.

In contrast, individual constant symbols should pick out a single element of D.

Consider `model1` as a way to implement a model with Standard ML, following the vocabulary given in (1) and using integers to represent entities of the model:

```
> model1 =
(7,
  fn "boy"          => [[0], [1]]
   | "girl"         => [[2]]
   | "person"       => [[0], [1], [2]]
   | "dog"          => [[3]]
   | "hill"         => [[4]]
   | "tree"         => [[5]]
   | "kite"         => [[6]]
   | "waves"        => [[1], [2]]
   | "is_namely"    => [[0,0], [1,1], [2,2], [3,3], [4,4], [5,5],
                        [6,6]]
   | "is_boy_on"    => [[0,4], [1,4]]
   | "is_girl_with" => [[2,3]]
   | "is_hill_with" => [[4,5]]
   | "flies"        => [[0,6]]
   | "sees"         => [[0,2], [0,3], [0,5], [1,2], [1,3], [1,5],
                        [2,0], [2,1], [2,4], [2,5], [3,2]]
   | "ren"          => [[0]]
   | "william"      => [[1]]
   | "yasuko"       => [[2]]
   | "rexx"         => [[3]]
```

```
   | _                    => raise (Error "unknown")
);
```
*val it = (7, fn): int * (string -> int list list)*

The feedback from Standard ML states that model1 consists of an integer, giving the size of the domain as 7 things to talk about, and an interpretation function mapping predicate names and constants (strings) into lists of lists of entities (integers). A list of all entities of the domain is obtained with List.tabulate and the identity function:

```
> List.tabulate (#1 model1, fn x => x);
```
val it = [0, 1, 2, 3, 4, 5, 6]: int list

Already the interpretation function allows checking whether relations hold true:

```
> member ([0, 3], #2 model1 "sees");
```
val it = true: bool

```
> member ([3, 0], #2 model1 "sees");
```
val it = false: bool

The semantic value for an individual constant symbol is the head of the head of the assigned list containing a single list containing a single integer.

```
> hd (hd (#2 model1 "rexx"));
```
val it = 3: int

1.2.2 The Semantics

This section introduces the semantics of first-order predicate logic by following Tarski's (1956) truth definition in the spirit of the textbook based implementations of Blackburn and Bos (2005) and van Eijck and Unger (2010). The truth definition ties together first-order languages and first-order models via an evaluation process that has the purpose to say whether a given predicate language expression is either *true* or *false* in a given model.

With a model of appropriate vocabulary, a sentence such as (2) is either true or false in the model.

```
(2)  Basic.QUANT ("∃", [Basic.X 1],
        Basic.REL ("waves", [Basic.X 1]))
```

More formally, there is a relation called *truth* which holds, or does not hold, between sentences and models of the same vocabulary. While it is often obvious whether a given sentence is true in a given model (e.g., truth for (2) holds if some waving individual is found in the model), arriving at a definition of this relation for arbitrary sentences is a challenge. In particular there can be no direct inductive definition of truth, for there are subexpressions of quantified sentences that are not sentences. For example, (2) is a sentence, but subexpression (3) is not.

(3) `Basic.REL ("waves", [Basic.X 1])`

An inductive truth definition defined solely in terms of sentences with respect to models could not explain why (2) is true or false in a model, since there would be no way to handle (3). Having a model is not enough; additional information is needed, specifically information on how to link the free variables to the entities in the model.

It is necessary to proceed indirectly. A three place relation called *satisfaction* is defined which holds between a model, an assignment of values to variables, and an expression. The assignment is a technical device to say what free variables stand for, and with this addition interpreting arbitrary expressions inductively is made possible.

An assignment that assigns every variable to the entity 0 can be implemented as `fn _ => 0`. This gives an interpretation to free variables, but only as denoting the fixed entity 0. Also required is an ability to consider *variants* of an assignment. Variant assignments are the technical tool that allows trying out new values for a given variable (say `Basic.X 1`) while keeping the values assigned to all other variables the same. An implementation of this idea is as follows:

```
fun variant (g, v, x) =
fn y =>
 if x = y then v else g y
```

Taking assignment g, domain entity v, and variable x as input, `variant` returns a variant of g that is like g in all respects, except that x is assigned the entity value of v. For example:

```
> (fn _ => 0) (Basic.X 1);
val it = 0: int
```

```
> (variant (fn _ => 0, 3, Basic.X 1)) (Basic.X 1);
val it = 3: int
```

```
> (variant (fn _ => 0, 3, Basic.X 1)) (Basic.X 2);
val it = 0: int
```

Let f be an expression, let m be a model, and let g be an assignment to variables of values in m, then the relation `FolSatisfy.eval (m, g, f)` can be implemented in Standard ML to say that f is satisfied in m with respect to the assignment of values to variables g.

```
structure FolSatisfy =
struct

fun eval (m: int * (string -> int list list), g: Basic.t -> int,
    f: Basic.t): bool =
 case f of
   Basic.REL ("∧", es) =>
    List.all (fn y => y = true) (map (fn e => eval (m, g, e)) es)
 | Basic.REL ("∨", es) =>
    List.exists
```

```
                (fn y => y = true) (map (fn e => eval (m, g, e)) es)
    | Basic.REL ("¬", [e]) => not (eval (m, g, e))
    | Basic.REL ("→", [e1, e2]) =>
        not ((eval (m, g, e1)) andalso not (eval (m, g, e2)))
    | Basic.REL (s, args) =>
        member (map (fn Basic.X n => g (Basic.X n)
                       | Basic.C s => hd (hd (#2 m s))
                       | _ => raise (Error "invalid term")) args,
                #2 m s)
    | Basic.QUANT ("∃", [x], e) =>
        List.exists (fn y => y = true) (
          List.tabulate
            (#1 m, fn v => eval (m, variant (g, v, x), e)))
    | Basic.QUANT ("∀", [x], e) =>
        List.all (fn y => y = true) (
          List.tabulate
            (#1 m, fn v => eval (m, variant (g, v, x), e)))
    | _ => raise (Error "invalid expression")
```

end

The evaluation of conjoined expressions, so matching Basic.REL (" ∧ ", es), where es is a list of subexpressions, proceeds by using map to apply fn e => eval (m, g, e) to each subexpression in es to return a list of bool values, and checking with List.all that all returned values are true; that is, truth holds for all the conjuncts.

The evaluation of disjoined expressions, so matching Basic.REL (" ∨ ", es), where es is a list of subexpressions, proceeds by using map to apply fn e => eval (m, g, e) to each subexpression in es to return a list of bool values, and checking with List.exists that there is a returned value that is true; that is, truth holds for at least one of the conjuncts.

The evaluation of negated expressions, so matching Basic.REL ("¬", [e]), where e is a subexpression, proceeds by obtaining the bool value from the evaluation of eval (m, g, e), and reversing the polarity of this value with the primitive Standard ML operator not, where:

> not true;
val it = false: bool

> not false;
val it = true: bool

The evaluation of expressions combined by implication, so matching Basic.REL (" → ", [e1, e2]), where e1 and e2 are subexpressions, proceeds by obtaining the bool values from the evaluations of eval (m, g, e1) and eval (m, g, e2), and calculating the resulting bool value with the primitive Standard ML operators not and andalso, where:

```
> not (true andalso not true);
val it = true: bool

> not (true andalso not false);
val it = false: bool

> not (false andalso not true);
val it = true: bool

> not (false andalso not false);
val it = true: bool
```

Remaining expressions that happen to match the pattern `Basic.REL (s, args)` are interpreted as atomic expressions. That is, a `bool` value is obtained by applying the interpretation function from the model #2 `m` to the predicate name `s` and checking whether the resulting semantic value contains the semantic value constructed from the arguments of the predicate. The latter is achieved by using `map` to apply a function for obtaining values for terms to each element of the list `args` to return a list of entity values.

In the remaining clauses for quantification, `variant` plays a crucial role. For the existential quantifier this boils down to: `Basic.QUANT ("∃", [x], e)` is satisfied in a given model with respect to an assignment `g` if and only if there is some domain entity `v` such that `variant (g, v, x)` satisfies `e` in the model. In other words, some value for the variable `x` should be found from the domain of the model that satisfies `e` in the model, while assignments to all other variables remain the same. This is implemented with the anonymous function `fn v => eval (m, variant (g, v, x), e)` which, when applied to an entity value, returns a `bool` value. The `bool` value returned is the result of evaluating the satisfaction of `e` with respect to `m` and a variant of `g` that assigns to `x` the entity value `v` obtained from the application. The created anonymous function is applied with `List.tabulate` to all the entities of the domain to return a list of `bool` values. If the returned list contains a single instance of `true`, then the satisfaction of `Basic.QUANT ("∃", [x], e)` will return `true`, else `false` is returned. In contrast, for the satisfaction of `Basic.QUANT ("∀", [x], e)` to return `true`, it must happen that every value in the returned list is `true`, else `false` is returned.

To demonstrate the satisfaction definition, here are some examples:

(4) A boy on a hill with a tree flies a kite.

```
> FolSatisfy.eval (model1, fn _ => 0,
    Basic.QUANT ("∃", [Basic.X 4],
     Basic.QUANT ("∃", [Basic.X 3],
      Basic.QUANT ("∃", [Basic.X 2],
       Basic.QUANT ("∃", [Basic.X 1],
        Basic.REL ("∧", [
         Basic.REL ("tree", [Basic.X 1]),
         Basic.REL ("is_hill_with", [Basic.X 2, Basic.X 1]),
```

```
              Basic.REL ("is_boy_on", [Basic.X 4, Basic.X 2]),
              Basic.REL ("kite", [Basic.X 3]),
              Basic.REL ("flies", [Basic.X 4, Basic.X 3])])))))));
val it = true: bool
```

(5) A boy, namely William, flies a kite.

```
> FolSatisfy.eval (model1, fn _ => 0,
    Basic.QUANT ("∃", [Basic.X 2],
      Basic.QUANT ("∃", [Basic.X 1],
        Basic.REL ("∧", [
          Basic.REL ("boy", [Basic.X 2]),
          Basic.REL ("kite", [Basic.X 1]),
          Basic.REL ("is_namely", [Basic.X 2, Basic.C "william"]),
          Basic.REL ("flies", [Basic.X 2, Basic.X 1])]))));
val it = false: bool
```

(6) Every boy sees a dog.

```
> FolSatisfy.eval (model1, fn _ => 0,
    Basic.QUANT ("∀", [Basic.X 1],
      Basic.REL ("→", [
        Basic.REL ("boy", [Basic.X 1]),
        Basic.QUANT ("∃", [Basic.X 2],
          Basic.REL ("∧", [
            Basic.REL ("dog", [Basic.X 2]),
            Basic.REL ("sees", [Basic.X 1, Basic.X 2])]))]))));
val it = true: bool
```

1.2.3 Truth Definition

With satisfaction, determining whether a sentence is true in a model can be defined:

- A sentence f is *true* in a model m = (dom, i) if and only if FolSatisfy.eval (m, g, f) returns true for any assignment g of values from dom to variables.

This definition of truth follows from the observation that it is of no consequence which assignment is used to compute the satisfaction of sentences. Sentences contain no free variables, so the only free variables encountered when evaluating a sentence are those produced when evaluating quantified subexpressions (if there are any). With such free variables the satisfaction definition will try out variants of the initial assignment state, so that the same results obtain irrespective of the initial state of the assignment.

1.3 A Target Language

To prepare the ground for the rest of the book, this section defines a general predicate language, `Lang.t`, that extends the `Basic.t` language. Relations (`Lang.REL`) and quantification (`Lang.QUANT`) have essentially identical `Basic.t` counterparts. Variables (`Lang.X`) and constants (`Lang.C`) have an extra string parameter to carry sort information for a *sorted* ontology (e.g., `"entity"`, `"group"`, `"attrib"`, `"degree"`, `"time"`, `"event"`, `"situation"`). Following Nakashima et al. (1996), there is a constructor (`Lang.At`) to state grammatical roles for expressions (`"event"`, `"arg0"`, `"arg1"`, `"arg2"`, `"of"`, `"h"` for nominal head, `"with"`, etc.). There are also new constructors (`Lang.Quant`, `Lang.QuantThrow` and `Lang.Throw`) that have parameters for information to reorganise the placement of expression content.

```
structure Lang =
struct

datatype t =
    C of string * string
  | X of int * string
  | REL of string * t list
  | QUANT of string * t list * t
  | At of t * string
  | Quant of string * string list * string * t list * t
  | QuantThrow of string * t * t
  | Throw of string * t

end
```

As an example, (7) might be coded as the `Lang.t` expression `ex3`.

(7) Yasuko doesn't see with her telescope the boys.

```
val ex3 =
Lang.Quant ("GROUP", ["event", "entity", "GROUP"], "∃",
 [Lang.X (1, "group")],
 Lang.Quant ("entity", ["event", "entity", "GROUP"], "∃", [],
  Lang.Quant ("event", ["event", "entity", "GROUP"], "∃", [],
   Lang.REL ("¬", [
    Lang.Quant ("entity", ["event", "entity"], "∃",
     [Lang.X (2, "entity")],
     Lang.Quant ("event", ["event", "entity"], "∃",
      [Lang.X (3, "event")],
      Lang.REL ("", [
       Lang.Throw ("entity",
        Lang.QuantThrow ("entity", Lang.X (4, "entity"),
         Lang.REL ("", [
```

```
                Lang.Throw ("entity",
                 Lang.REL ("her:pick", [
                   Lang.X (4, "entity"), Lang.C ("yasuko", "entity")])),
                 Lang.REL ("telescope", [
                  Lang.At (Lang.X (2, "entity"), "h"),
                  Lang.At (Lang.X (4, "entity"), "of")])])]))),
           Lang.REL ("", [
            Lang.Throw ("GROUP",
             Lang.REL ("boys", [
              Lang.At (Lang.X (1, "group"), "h")])),
            Lang.REL ("does_see", [
             Lang.At (Lang.X (3, "event"), "event"),
             Lang.At (Lang.C ("yasuko", "entity"), "arg0"),
             Lang.At (Lang.X (1, "group"), "arg1"),
             Lang.At (Lang.X (2, "entity"), "with")])])])))])))))
```

The main predicate "does_see" has four arguments, each formed with Lang.At to specify grammatical role: "event", "arg0", "arg1", and "with" (an adjunct binding). A fixed order to argument placement is unnecessary with such coding of grammatical information. The nominal predicate "telescope" has two arguments: "h" needing to be a telescope, and "of" the telescope possessor. The nominal predicate "boys" has an "h" argument binding only. By contrast ordering is important with "her:pick": the first argument should be equated with a following argument to achieve pronoun resolution.

Forming restriction materials, the "her:pick" condition and the nominal predicates of "telescope" and "boys" each fall under a Lang.Throw (sort, _) instance, where sort is the sort of the value to which the restriction applies, e.g., "boys" is within the scope of Lang.Throw ("GROUP", _). The quantification that binds the first argument of "her:pick" happens with Lang.QuantThrow while all other quantifications are brought about by Lang.Quant. Also note that Lang.REL ("",_) is employed as a default for having structure without specifying a relation.

1.3.1 Post-processing

The purpose of Lang.Quant, Lang.QuantThrow and Lang.Throw is to support repositioning expression material. This is accomplished by passing Lang.t expressions to the post-processing routine Post.transform. The result is an expression with materials possibly repositioned, instances of Lang.Quant replaced by Lang.QUANT, and instances of Lang.QuantThrow and Lang.Throw eliminated. Post.format is recursively defined together with Post.trans, the main routine that integrates with instances of Lang.Quant collected bindings and collected conditions, Post.bindings, a routine to collect bindings launched for repositioning with instances of Lang.QuantThrow, and Post.conditions, a routine to collect conditions launched with instances of Lang.Throw.

```
structure Post =
struct

fun transform (f: Lang.t): Lang.t =
 let
  val result = trans f
 in
  if length result = 1 then hd result else Lang.REL ("", result)
 end
and trans (f: Lang.t): Lang.t list =
 case f of
   Lang.REL (s, es) =>
    let
     val res = List.concat (map trans es)
    in
     if s = "" andalso length res = 1 then
      case res of
        Lang.At (Lang.C _, _)::nil => nil
      | Lang.At (Lang.X _, _)::nil => nil
      | _ => res
     else
      [Lang.REL (s, res)]
    end
 | Lang.QUANT (s, xs, e) =>
    if null xs andalso member (s, ["∃", "∀"]) then [transform e]
    else [Lang.QUANT (s, xs, transform e)]
 | Lang.At (e, s) => [Lang.At (transform e, s)]
 | Lang.Quant (y, ys, s, xs, e) =>
    let
     val bnd = bindings (y, e)
     val cnd = List.concat (map (fn z => conditions (z, e)) ys)
     val main =
      if null cnd then
       transform e
      else
       Lang.REL ((fn "∃" => "∧" | "∀" => "→" | _ => "") s,
        cnd @ [transform e])
    in
     if null (xs @ bnd) andalso member (s, ["∃", "∀"]) then [main]
     else
      [Lang.QUANT (s, xs @ bnd, main)]
    end
```

```
    | Lang.QuantThrow (_, _, e) => trans e
    | Lang.Throw _ => nil
    | _ => [f]
and bindings (x: string, f: Lang.t): Lang.t list =
  case f of
      Lang.REL (_, es) =>
        List.concat (map (fn e => bindings (x, e)) es)
    | Lang.QUANT (_, _, e) => bindings (x, e)
    | Lang.At (e, _) => bindings (x, e)
    | Lang.Quant (y, _, _, _, e) =>
        if x = y then nil else bindings (x, e)
    | Lang.QuantThrow (y, b, e) =>
        if x = y then [b] @ bindings (x, e) else bindings (x, e)
    | Lang.Throw (_, e) => bindings (x, e)
    | _ => nil
and conditions (x: string, f: Lang.t): Lang.t list =
  case f of
      Lang.REL (_, es) =>
        List.concat (map (fn e => conditions (x, e)) es)
    | Lang.QUANT (_, _, e) => conditions (x, e)
    | Lang.At (e, _) => conditions (x, e)
    | Lang.Quant (_, ys, _, _, e) =>
        if member (x, ys) then nil else conditions (x, e)
    | Lang.QuantThrow (_, _, e) => conditions (x, e)
    | Lang.Throw (y, e) =>
        if x = y then conditions (x, e) @ [transform e]
        else conditions (x, e)
    | _ => nil

end
```

For a demonstration, ex3 can be sent to Post.transform:

```
> Post.transform ex3;
val it =
QUANT ("∃", [X (1, "group")],
 REL ("∧", [REL ("boys", [At (X (1, "group"), "h")]),
  REL ("¬", [
   QUANT ("∃", [X (2, "entity"), X (4, "entity")],
    QUANT ("∃", [X (3, "event")],
     REL ("∧", [
      REL ("her:pick", [X (4, "entity"), C ("yasuko", "entity")]),
      REL ("telescope", [At (X (2, "entity"), "h"), At (X (4, "entity"), "of")]),
      REL ("does_see", [At (X (3, "event"), "event"),
       At (C ("yasuko", "entity"), "arg0"), At (X (1, "group"), "arg1"),
```

At (X (2, "entity"), "with")])])))])])
: Lang.t

Note that, in reorganising the placement of expression content, `Post.transform` eliminates the constructors of `Lang.t` with parameters for reorganising information (`Lang.Quant`, `Lang.QuantThrow` and `Lang.Throw`).

1.3.2 Davidsonian Representations

This section considers further processing of `Lang.t` expressions to derive representations associated with Davidsonian event semantics (Davidson 1967; Parsons 1990; Landman 2000). This involves fixing grammatical roles to arity positions, or when this is not possible either adding conditions as modifiers of event variables or adapting predicates to support extra fixed arity positions. For example,

```
Lang.REL ("does_see", [
 Lang.At (Lang.X (3, "event"), "event"),
 Lang.At (Lang.C ("yasuko", "entity"), "arg0"),
 Lang.At (Lang.X (1, "group"), "arg1"),
 Lang.At (Lang.X (2, "entity"), "with")])
```

changes to:

```
REL ("∧", [
 REL ("does_see", [
  X (3, "event"), C ("yasuko", "entity"), X (1, "group")]),
 REL ("=", [
  REL ("with", [X (3, "event")]),
  X (2, "entity")])])
```

while:

```
Lang.REL ("telescope", [
 Lang.At (Lang.X (2, "entity"), "h"),
 Lang.At (Lang.X (4, "entity"), "of")])
```

changes to:

```
REL ("is_telescope_of", [X (2, "entity"), X (4, "entity")])
```

Such conversion is implemented with `Davidsonian.format`:

```
structure Davidsonian =
struct

val nix = Lang.C ("_", "_")
```

```
fun argnt (role: string, l: Lang.t list): Lang.t =
 case l of
   nil => nix
 | Lang.At (e, s)::r => if s = role then e else argnt (role, r)
 | _::r => argnt (role, r)

fun rmArg (xs: string list, l: Lang.t list): Lang.t list =
 case l of
   nil => nil
 | Lang.At (e, s)::r =>
    if member (s, xs) then rmArg (xs, r)
    else Lang.At (e, s)::rmArg (xs, r)
 | h::r => h::rmArg (xs, r)

fun format (f: Lang.t): Lang.t =
 case f of
   Lang.QUANT (s, x, f) => Lang.QUANT (s, x, format f)
 | Lang.Quant (c, l, oper, x, f) =>
    Lang.Quant (c, l, oper, x, format f)
 | Lang.QuantThrow (c, x, f) => Lang.QuantThrow (c, x, format f)
 | Lang.REL (s, es) =>
    let
     val res = diff (es, [Lang.REL ("", nil)])
     val event = if argnt ("event", res) <> nix then
      argnt ("event", res) else argnt ("EVENT", res)
     val fact = argnt ("fact", res)
     val h = argnt ("h", res)
    in
     if event <> nix then
      let
       val embed = diff (
        map (fn x => format (argnt (x, res)))
         ["that", "toComp"], [nix])
       val rst = rmArg (
        ["event", "EVENT", "that", "toComp"], res)
       val arg2 = argnt ("arg2", rst)
       val arg1 = argnt ("arg1", rst)
       val arg0 = argnt ("arg0", rst)
       val attr = argnt ("attribute", rst)
       val main =
        if arg2 <> nix then
         [format event, format arg0] @
         (if
           arg1 = nix andalso not (null embed)
          then
```

```
            embed @ [format arg2]
          else
            [format arg1, format arg2] @ embed)
        else if arg1 <> nix then
          [format event, format arg0, format arg1] @ embed
        else if attr <> nix then
          [format event, format arg0, format attr] @ embed
        else if arg0 <> nix then
          [format event, format arg0] @ embed
        else [format event] @ embed
      val mods =
        if arg2 <> nix then rmArg (["arg0", "arg1", "arg2"], rst)
        else if arg1 <> nix then rmArg (["arg0", "arg1"], rst)
        else if attr <> nix then rmArg (["arg0", "attribute"], rst)
        else if arg0 <> nix then rmArg (["arg0"], rst)
        else rst
    in
      if null mods then
        Lang.REL (s, main)
      else
        Lang.REL ("∧", [Lang.REL (s, main)] @
          map (fn x => argBlock (format event, x)) mods)
      end
    else if fact <> nix orelse h <> nix then
      let
        val main = if fact <> nix then fact else h
        val mods = if fact <> nix then
          rmArg (["fact"], res) else rmArg (["h"], res)
      in
        if null mods then
          Lang.REL (s, [format main])
        else if length mods = 1 then
          hd (map (fn x => relBlock (s, main, x)) mods)
        else
          Lang.REL ("∧", map (fn x => relBlock (s, main, x)) mods)
      end
    else
      Lang.REL (s, map format res)
    end
  | Lang.At (e, _) => format e
  | Lang.Throw (x, e) => Lang.Throw (x, format e)
  | _ => f
and argBlock (h: Lang.t, x: Lang.t): Lang.t =
  if (fn Lang.At _ => false | _ => true) x then
    format x
```

```
        else
          Lang.REL ("=", [
            Lang.REL ((fn Lang.At (_, s) => s | _ => "_") x,
              [format h]),
            format x])
    and relBlock (s: string, h: Lang.t, x: Lang.t): Lang.t =
      if (fn Lang.At _ => false | _ => true) x then
        format x
      else
        Lang.REL
          ("is_" ^ s ^ (fn Lang.At (_, s) => "_" ^ s | _ => "") x,
            [format h, format x])

end
```

As an example, consider processing ex3:

```
> Davidsonian.format (Post.transform ex3);
val it =
QUANT ("∃", [X (1, "group")],
 REL ("∧", [REL ("boys", [X (1, "group")]),
  REL ("¬", [
   QUANT ("∃", [X (2, "entity"), X (4, "entity")],
   QUANT ("∃", [X (3, "event")],
    REL ("∧", [
     REL ("her:pick", [X (4, "entity"), C ("yasuko", "entity")]),
     REL ("is_telescope_of", [X (2, "entity"), X (4, "entity")]),
     REL ("∧", [
     REL ("does_see", [X (3, "event"), C ("yasuko", "entity"),
      X (1, "group")]),
      REL ("=", [REL ("with", [X (3, "event")]), X (2, "entity")])])]))])]))
: Lang.t
```

Notably all instances of Lang.At are eliminated. A pretty print of the result from post-processing is as follows:

$$\exists X_1 (boys (X_1) \ \wedge$$
$$\neg \ \exists x_4 x_2 e_3 (x_4 = her\{yasuko\} \ \wedge \ is\_telescope\_of(x_2, \ x_4) \ \wedge$$
$$does\_see(e_3, \ yasuko, \ X_1) \ \wedge \ with(e_3) \ = \ x_2))$$

It follows that the consequence of processing with both Post.transform of Sect. 1.3.1 and Davidsonian.format of this section is that transformation is to expressions of the subset of the Lang.t language that have Basic.t language counterparts.

1.4 Summary

The aim of this chapter has been to specify what a predicate language is in syntactic terms and to present model-theoretic semantic methods by defining how satisfaction (*truth*) of a predicate language expression in a first-order model can be checked with respect to an assignment function. Subsequent chapters will progressively develop the evaluation techniques that underlie the definition of satisfaction, only with limitation to the aim of realising mechanisms for returning predicate language expressions (specifically, Lang.t expressions) as representations of meanings derived by evaluation from inputs that are ultimately conventional phrase structure parsings of natural language.

References

Barendregt HP (1984) The Lambda calculus: its syntax and semantics. North-Holland, Amsterdam

Blackburn P, Bos J (2005) Representation and inference for natural language: a first course in computational semantics. Studies in computational linguistics. CSLI Publications, Stanford

Davidson D (1967) The logical form of action sentences. In: Rescher N (ed) The logic of decision and action. University of Pittsburgh Press, Pittsburgh. Reprinted in: Davidson D (1980) Essays on actions and events. Clarendon Press, Oxford, pp 105–122

Landman F (2000) Events and plurality: the Jerusalem lectures. Kluwer Academic Publishers, Dordrecht

Milner R, Tofte M, Harper R, MacQueen D (1997) The definition of standard ML (revised). MIT Press, Cambridge

Nakashima H, Noda I, Kenichi H (1996) Organic programming language GAEA for multi-agents. In: Proceedings of the second international conference on multiagent systems (ICMAS-96). AAAI

Parsons T (1990) Events in the semantics of English. MIT Press, Cambridge

Tarski A (1956) The concept of truth in formalized languages. In: Logic, semantics, metamathematics. Clarendon Press, Oxford

van Eijck J, Unger C (2010) Computational semantics with functional programming. Cambridge University Press, Cambridge

Chapter 2
Self-Selective Evaluation

"Suppose someone to assert:

The gostak distims the doshes.

You do not know what this means; nor do I. But if we assume that it is English, we know that the doshes are distimmed by the gostak. We know too that one distimmer of doshes is a gostak. If, moreover, the doshes are galloons, we know that some galloons are distimmed by the gostak. And so we may go on, and so we often do go on." (Richards and Ogden 1923)

The departure point for this chapter is a recursive routine for evaluating expressions against an assignment function that stores accumulated binding information for binding names (of which the classical interpretation of predicate logic in Sect. 1.2 is one example). An If conditional operation is added so that what is evaluated can be automatically selected during the runtime of evaluation based on tests regarding the state of the assignment function. This new operation is demonstrated to be an essential component for enabling a robust interpretation of unknown lexical items and for feeding an automated regulation of binding information to leave little need for explicitly coding dependencies.

The chapter is organised as follows. Section 2.1 introduces sequence assignments. Section 2.2 presents the 'a Self.t language, with an evaluation routine for reaching Lang.t expressions. The 'a Self.t language is of interest because it includes the conditional Self.If, as well as other operations that exploit the additional structure present with a sequence assignment (notably Self.Lam and Self.Clean). Section 2.3 links the 'a Self.t language to natural language data. Section 2.4 offers a summary. The purpose of creating and exploring the 'a Self.t language and so for this chapter is to prepare the ground for introducing the more capable 'a Sct.t language of Chap. 3.

© Springer International Publishing Switzerland 2015
A. Butler, *Linguistic Expressions and Semantic Processing*,
DOI 10.1007/978-3-319-18830-0_2

2.1 Sequence Assignments

Having an If conditional such that what is evaluated can be selected based on the state of the assignment function is of utility with an assignment function that has sufficient properties to test. Typically assignment functions with the least amount of structure possible are favoured in order to limit assumptions. For example the assignment function for classical interpretations of predicate logic, as seen in Sect. 1.2, assigns to all variables a (possibly different) single value. This offers nothing to test, beyond assigned values being specific values.

In a series of papers Vermeulen (1993, 2000) and Hollenberg and Vermeulen (1996) propose an altogether richer assignment function in which (possibly empty) sequences (or stacks) of values are assigned to variables. Assignments with such additional structure are utilised in the evaluation systems of, for example, Visser and Vermeulen (1996), van Eijck (2001), Dekker (2002, 2012) and Butler (2007, 2010). With a sequence assignment, in addition to assigned values being specific sequences, it is possible to test for sequence length.

Having sequence assignments allows for operations to add (Assign.push), remove (Assign.pop and Assign.popLast) and manipulate (Assign.shiftLast and Assign.manage) assigned content. The following Standard ML implementation has the assignment type 'a assign made polymorphic with regards to the type 'a list of values assigned to strings. Empty exceptions are raised if operations fail.

```
structure Assign =
struct

type 'a t = string -> 'a list

fun push (d: 'a, x: string, g: 'a t): 'a t =
fn y =>
 if x = y then [d] @ g y else g y

fun pop (x: string, g: 'a t):  'a t =
fn y =>
 if x = y then tl (g x) else g y

fun popLast (x: string, g: 'a t):  'a t =
fn y =>
 if x = y then List.take (g x, length (g x)-1) else g y

val shiftLast: string -> string -> 'a t -> 'a t =
fn x => fn y => fn g =>
 popLast (x, push (List.last (g x), y, g))
```

```
fun manage (n: int, xs: string list, y: string, g: 'a t): 'a t =
  case xs of
    nil => g
  | x::r =>
      manage (n, r, y, iterate (shiftLast x y) (length (g x)-n) g)
end
```

The empty assignment is `fn _ => nil`, which maps every binding name to the empty list.

`Assign.push` returns a variant of `g` differing only in that `d` is added as the first element of the sequence assigned `x`. For example:

```
> (Assign.push (2, "arg0",
      Assign.push (1, "arg0", fn _ => nil))) "arg0";
val it = [2, 1]: int list
```

`Assign.pop` returns `g` except with the first sequence element assigned `x` removed. For example:

```
> (Assign.pop ("arg0",
      Assign.push (2, "arg0",
        Assign.push (1, "arg0", fn _ => nil)))) "arg0";
val it = [1]: int list
```

`Assign.popLast` returns `g` except with the last sequence element assigned `x` removed. For example:

```
> (Assign.popLast ("arg0",
      Assign.push (2, "arg0",
        Assign.push (1, "arg0", fn _ => nil)))) "arg0";
val it = [2]: int list
```

`Assign.shiftLast` returns `g` except with the last sequence element assigned `x` removed (by `Assign.popLast`) and made (by `Assign.push`) the new first sequence element assigned `y`. For example:

```
> val g = Assign.shiftLast "arg0" "c"
    (fn "arg0" => [4, 3, 2] | "c" => [1] | _ => nil);
val g = fn: int Assign.t
```

```
> g "arg0";
val it = [4, 3]: int list
```

```
> g "c";
val it = [2, 1]: int list
```

`Assign.manage` returns an assignment while taking as input:

1. integer n,
2. xs of type `string list`,

3. y of type `string` and
4. assignment `g`.

The returned assignment is a variant of `g` in having been possibly altered by (multiple applications of) `shiftLast`, which takes a string from `xs` as the value for its first parameter and the string `y` as the value for its second parameter. Exact applications of `shiftLast` are determined with `iterate` (re)applying `shiftLast` based on a number calculated by subtracting the integer value `n` from the length of the sequence assigned to the string value from `xs`.

   `Assign.manage` can be demonstrated as follows:

```
> val g = fn "arg0" => [2, 1] | "arg1" => [5, 4, 3] | _ => nil;
```
val g = fn: int Assign.t

```
> g "arg0";
```
val it = [2, 1]: int list

```
> g "arg1";
```
val it = [5, 4, 3]: int list

```
> g "c";
```
val it = []: int list

```
> val h = Assign.manage (1, ["arg0", "arg1"], "c", g);
```
val h = fn: int Assign.t

```
> h "arg0";
```
val it = [2]: int list

```
> h "arg1";
```
val it = [5]: int list

```
> h "c";
```
val it = [4, 3, 1]: int list

2.2 Self Language

The `'a Self.t` datatype defines the `'a Self.t` language. Function `Self.names` of type `'a Self.t -> string list` extracts to a list the binding names of an `'a Self.t` expression.

```
structure Self =
struct

datatype 'a t =
   T of string
```

```
    | Some of string * 'a t
    | Rel of string * 'a t list
    | If of ('a Assign.t -> bool) * 'a t * 'a t
    | Lam of string * string * 'a t
    | Clean of int * string list * string * 'a t
    | Names of string list -> 'a t

fun names (f: 'a t): string list =
  case f of
    T x => [x]
  | Some (x, e) => uniq ([x] @ names e)
  | Rel (_, es) => uniq (List.concat (map names es))
  | If (_, e1, e2) => uniq (names e1 @ names e2)
  | Lam (x, y, e) => uniq ([x, y] @ names e)
  | Clean (_, xs, _, e) => uniq (xs @ names e)
  | Names func => names (func nil)

end
```

Evaluation for the 'a Self.t language will be illustrated with the implementation of an evaluation routine, SelfToLang.eval, that is relativised against Lang.t Assign.t assignments and transforms Lang.t Self.t expressions into Lang.t expressions.

In transforming to Lang.t expressions, to ensure the Barendregt variable convention (see Sect. 1.1.3) is obeyed by the resulting Lang.t expression, it is important to ensure freshness for created variables of the Lang.t language that are added to sequences that serve as values assigned to Lang.t Self.t binding names. This is achieved with reference to SelfToLang.cnt, which has an initial state of 0.

```
structure SelfToLang =
struct

val cnt = ref 0;

fun env (x: string, g: Lang.t Assign.t): Lang.t Assign.t =
  (inc cnt ;
   Assign.push (
   Lang.X (!cnt, if x = "event" then x else "entity"), x, g))


fun eval (g: Lang.t Assign.t, f: Lang.t Self.t): Lang.t =
  let
    fun evaluate (l, g, f) =
      case f of
        Self.T x => Lang.At (hd (g x), x)
      | Self.Some (x, e) =>
          let
```

```
              val h = env (x, g)
          in
            Lang.QUANT ("∃", [hd (h x)], evaluate (1, h, e))
          end
      | Self.Rel (s, es) =>
          Lang.REL (s, map (fn e => evaluate (1, g, e)) es)
      | Self.If (func, e1, e2) =>
          if func g then evaluate (1, g, e1) else evaluate (1, g, e2)
      | Self.Lam (x, y, e) =>
          evaluate
            (1, Assign.pop (x, Assign.push (hd (g x), y, g)), e)
      | Self.Clean (n, xs, y, e) =>
          evaluate (1, Assign.manage (n, xs, y, g), e)
      | Self.Names func => evaluate (1, g, func 1)
  in
    evaluate (Self.names f, g, f)
  end

end
```

Content is added to an assignment (that may be the empty assignment) with SelfToLang.env. Taking a string x and assignment g as parameters, SelfToLang.env treats x as a binding name, for which a fresh term is created as the new first assigned value. If the binding name is "event" then the added value is an event variable of Lang.t, otherwise the added value is an individual variable of Lang.t. For example:

```
> val g = SelfToLang.env ("event",
    SelfToLang.env ("event",
    SelfToLang.env ("arg0", fn _ => nil)));
val g = fn: Lang.t Assign.t
```

```
> g "event";
val it = [X (3, "event"), X (2, "event")]: Lang.t list
```

```
> g "arg0";
val it = [X (1, "entity")]: Lang.t list
```

Evaluation of term Self.T x returns a Lang.At role value construct (see Sect. 1.3.1) with the first element of the sequence assigned x as value and the name x to indicate grammatical role. An Empty exception is raised with failure. For example:

```
> SelfToLang.eval (
    fn "arg0" => [Lang.X (2, "entity"), Lang.X (1, "entity")]
    | _ => nil,
    Self.T "arg0");
val it = At (X (2, "entity"), "arg0"): Lang.t
```

```
> SelfToLang.eval (fn _ => nil, Self.T "arg0");
```
Exception- Empty raised

The quantifier `Self.Some` (x, e) adds one new value to the sequence assigned x and returns `Lang.QUANT` with ∃ to (i) bind as a variable the newly introduced value and (ii) scope over the evaluation of e against the adjusted assignment. For example:

```
> SelfToLang.eval (fn _ => nil,
    Self.Some ("arg0", Self.T "arg0"));
```
val it = QUANT ("∃", [X (1, "entity")], At (X (1, "entity"), "arg0")): Lang.t

Changes to the assignment that occur can be pictured as follows:

empty assignment
|

```
Self.Some ("arg0", _): Lang.QUANT("∃", [X (1, "entity")], _)
          [ "arg0" → [X (1, "entity")] ]
```

|

```
            Self.T "arg0":
     Lang.At (X (1, "entity"), "arg0")
```

Beginning from the empty assignment a fresh value `Lang.X` (1, "entity") is entered as a value of the sequence assigned "arg0", and serves as the bound value for the role value construct returned with the evaluation of `Self.T` "arg0".

Evaluation of `Self.Rel` (s, es) against assignment g returns a relation s that has the evaluation of nth expression of es against g as the nth argument. For example:

```
> SelfToLang.eval (
    fn "arg0" => [Lang.X (1, "entity")] | _ => nil,
    Self.Rel ("", [Self.T "arg0", Self.T "arg0"]));
```
val it =
REL ("", [At (X (1, "entity"), "arg0"), At (X (1, "entity"), "arg0")])
: Lang.t

`Self.If` takes `Lang.t Assign.t -> bool` function func to test the current assignment state and two `Lang.t Self.t` expressions, e1 and e2. If func applied to the assignment returns `true`, e1 is evaluated, else e2 is evaluated. For example:

```
> SelfToLang.eval (
    fn "arg0" => [Lang.X (1, "entity")] | _ => nil,
    Self.If (fn g: Lang.t Assign.t => null (g "arg1"),
      Self.T "arg0", Self.T "arg1"));
```
val it = At (X (1, "entity"), "arg0"): Lang.t

The test returns `true`, so `Self.T` "arg0" is evaluated.

$$\left[\,\text{"arg0"} \rightarrow [\text{X} \ (1, \ \text{"entity"})]\,\right]$$

$$\big|$$

```
        Self.If is true: _
            Self.T "arg0":
Lang.At (X (1, "entity"), "arg0")
```

With a different assignment state the test can return `false`, so `Self.T "arg1"` is evaluated.

```
> SelfToLang.eval (
    fn "arg0" => [Lang.X (1, "entity")]
    | "arg1" => [Lang.X (2, "entity")]
    | _ => nil,
    Self.If (fn g: Lang.t Assign.t => null (g "arg1"),
      Self.T "arg0", Self.T "arg1"));
val it = At (X (2, "entity"), "arg1"): Lang.t
```

$$\left[\begin{array}{l}\text{"arg0"} \rightarrow [\text{X} \ (1, \ \text{"entity"})] \\ \text{"arg1"} \rightarrow [\text{X} \ (2, \ \text{"entity"})]\end{array}\right]$$

$$\big|$$

```
        Self.If is false: _
            Self.T "arg1":
Lang.At (X (2, "entity"), "arg1")
```

`Self.Lam (x, y, e)` returns the evaluation of e against assignment g modified with `Assign.pop (x, Assign.push (hd (g x), y, g))`. For example:

```
> SelfToLang.eval (
    fn "arg0" => [Lang.X (2, "entity"), Lang.X (3, "entity")]
    | "h" => [Lang.X (1, "entity")]
    | _ => nil,
    Self.Lam ("arg0", "h", Self.T "h"));
val it = At (X (2, "entity"), "h"): Lang.t
```

$$\begin{bmatrix} \text{"arg0"} \to [\text{X (2, "entity"), X (3, "entity")}] \\ \text{"h"} \to [\text{X (1, "entity")}] \end{bmatrix}$$

$$|$$

$$\text{Self.Lam ("arg0", "h", \_): \_}$$
$$\begin{bmatrix} \text{"arg0"} \to [\text{X (3, "entity")}] \\ \text{"h"} \to [\text{X (2, "entity"), X (1, "entity")}] \end{bmatrix}$$

$$|$$

$$\text{Self.T "h":}$$
$$\text{Lang.At (X (2, "entity"), "h")}$$

That is, evaluation of Self.T "h" takes place against an assignment state where what had been the first element of the sequence assigned "arg0" is repositioned to be the first element of the sequence assigned "h".

Self.Clean (n, xs, y, e) modifies the assignment with Assign.manage (n, xs, y), and returns the evaluation of e against the altered assignment. Consequently potentially multiple values from the sequences assigned to the names of xs are reallocated with shiftLast into the sequence assigned y, with the consequence that sequences with n elements remain assigned to each xs name. For example:

```
> SelfToLang.eval (
    fn "h" => [Lang.X (2, "entity"), Lang.X (3, "entity")]
    | _ => nil,
    Self.Clean (1, ["h"], "c", Self.T "h"));
val it = At (X (2, "entity"), "h"): Lang.t
```

$$\begin{bmatrix} \text{"h"} \to [\text{X (2, "entity"), X (3, "entity")}] \end{bmatrix}$$

$$|$$

$$\text{Self.Clean (1, ["h"], "c", \_): \_}$$
$$\begin{bmatrix} \text{"h"} \to [\text{X (2, "entity")}] \\ \text{"c"} \to [\text{X (3, "entity")}] \end{bmatrix}$$

$$|$$

$$\text{Self.T "h":}$$
$$\text{Lang.At (X (2, "entity"), "h")}$$

Self.Clean has the effect of an operation of 'unbinding' like in Berkling (1976) and still more like the 'end-of-scope' operator in Hendriks and van Oostrom (2003) since Self.Clean is not limited to the terminal level. A notable difference is that binding values are not destroyed but rather gathered as values of the sequence assigned to the name of the y parameter, which is employed in Chap. 3. to make antecedents accessible for pronouns.

Self.Names is an operation to feed func of type string list -> 'a Self.t a list of binding names gathered with self.names applied when evaluation starts. For example:

```
> SelfToLang.eval (
    fn _ => nil,
    Self.Some ("arg0",
     Self.Some ("arg1",
      Self.Names (fn l =>
       Self.Rel ("", map (fn x => Self.T x) l)))));
```

val it =
QUANT ("∃", [X (1, "entity")],
 QUANT ("∃", [X (2, "entity")],
  REL ("", [At (X (1, "entity"), "arg0"), At (X (2, "entity"), "arg1")])))
: Lang.t

2.3 Applying the Self Language

The purpose of this section is to illustrate links of the 'a Self.t language to natural language data. Section 2.3.1 applies the 'a Self.t language to capture verbs with core arguments ("arg0" and "arg1" bindings). Section 2.3.2 adds encodings for nouns. Coverage is extended further in Sect. 2.3.3 to include non-core bindings.

2.3.1 Core Arguments

As a first application of the 'a Self.t language, consider the task of simulating how differing presences of noun phrases influence processing the pseudoverb *distims* in (1). For (1a) to be a well-formed sentence, *distims* ought to be an intransitive verb; for (1b), a transitive verb; and for (1c), a verb without bound arguments (e.g., *rains*).

(1) a. Someone distims.
    b. Someone distims someone.
    c. It distims.

The data of (1) can be captured with a method to handle the core grammatical roles of subject and object. Suppose grammatical subjects are established with "arg0" bindings, while grammatical objects involve "arg1" bindings. The noun phrase *someone* should create either "arg0" or "arg1" bindings, while the verb *distims* should bring about predicate encodings with appropriate "arg0" and "arg1" bound arguments.

Absence or presence of an "arg0" binding can be used as the basis for selecting whether *someone* creates an "arg0" or "arg1" binding.

```
val SOMEONE =
fn e =>
 Self.If (fn g: Lang.t Assign.t => null (g "arg0"),
  Self.Some ("arg0", e),
  Self.Some ("arg1", e))
```

Consider `verb1` as an initial attempt at an operation for constructing verbs from strings:

```
val verb1 =
fn s =>
 Self.Some ("event",
  Self.If (fn g: Lang.t Assign.t => null (g "arg0"),
   Self.Rel (s, [Self.T "event"]),
   Self.If (fn g: Lang.t Assign.t => null (g "arg1"),
    Self.Rel (s, [Self.T "event", Self.T "arg0"]),
    Self.Rel
     (s, [Self.T "event", Self.T "arg0", Self.T "arg1"])))))
```

Encodings for the examples of (1) as `Lang.t Self.t` expressions can now be offered as follows:

```
val ex1 = SOMEONE (verb1 "distims")
```

```
val ex2 = SOMEONE (SOMEONE (verb1 "distims"))
```

```
val ex3 = verb1 "distims"
```

Evaluations result in `Lang.t` expressions, with generated bound arguments appearing alongside information about the grammatical role of the argument:

```
> SelfToLang.eval (fn _ => nil, ex1);
```
val it =
QUANT ("∃", [X (1, "entity")],
 QUANT ("∃", [X (2, "event")],
  REL ("distims", [At (X (2, "event"), "event"), At (X (1, "entity"), "arg0")])))
: Lang.t

```
> SelfToLang.eval (fn _ => nil, ex2);
```
val it =
QUANT ("∃", [X (1, "entity")],
 QUANT ("∃", [X (2, "entity")],
  QUANT ("∃", [X (3, "event")],
   REL ("distims", [At (X (3, "event"), "event"), At (X (1, "entity"), "arg0"),
    At (X (2, "entity"), "arg1")]))))
: Lang.t

```
> SelfToLang.eval (fn _ => nil, ex3);
```
val it =

QUANT ("∃", [X (1, "event")], REL ("distims", [At (X (1, "event"), "event")]))
: Lang.t

Three different forms for the verb `"distims"` arise, all of which have a bound argument with an `"event"` role while varying as to whether there are bound arguments
with `"arg0"` and `"arg1"` roles. Notably, evaluation of `ex1` produces an intransitive
verb encoding for `"distims"`, evaluation of `ex2` produces a transitive verb encoding,
and evaluation of `ex3` produces a verb encoding without bound arguments.

To see why the results obtain, consider `ex2` in detail. Executing `ex2` at the Standard
ML prompt results in the following reduced `Lang.t Self.t` expression:

```
> ex2;
```
val it =
If (fn,
 Some ("arg0",
 If (fn,
 Some ("arg0",
  Some ("event",
  If (fn, Rel ("distims", [T "event"]),
   If (fn, Rel ("distims", [T "event", T "arg0"]),
    Rel ("distims", [T "event", T "arg0", T "arg1"]))))),
  Some ("arg1",
  Some ("event",
  If (fn, Rel ("distims", [T "event"]),
   If (fn, Rel ("distims", [T "event", T "arg0"]),
    Rel ("distims", [T "event", T "arg0", T "arg1"])))))))),
 Some ("arg1",
 If (fn,
 Some ("arg0",
  Some ("event",
  If (fn, Rel ("distims", [T "event"]),
   If (fn, Rel ("distims", [T "event", T "arg0"]),
    Rel ("distims", [T "event", T "arg0", T "arg1"]))))),
  Some ("arg1",
  Some ("event",
  If (fn, Rel ("distims", [T "event"]),
   If (fn, Rel ("distims", [T "event", T "arg0"]),
    Rel ("distims", [T "event", T "arg0", T "arg1"])))))))))
: Lang.t Self.t

The resulting `Lang.t Self.t` expression consists of a series of `Self.If` conditionals, with evaluation navigating a particular route through the conditionals to
determine the form of the `Lang.t` expression that is returned, as the following chart
illustrates.

SOMEONE	SOMEONE	verb1 "distims"		
null "arg0"?	null "arg0"?	null "arg0"?	null "arg1"?	arguments
		Yes		"event"
	Yes: create "arg0"	No	Yes	"event","arg0"
			No	"event","arg0","arg1"
Yes: create "arg0"		Yes		"event"
	No: create "arg1"	No	Yes	"event","arg0"
			No	"event","arg0","arg1"
		Yes		"event"
	Yes: create "arg0"	No	Yes	"event","arg0"
			No	"event","arg0","arg1"
No: create "arg1"		Yes		"event"
	No: create "arg1"	No	Yes	"event","arg0"
			No	"event","arg0","arg1"

The following picture depicts states of the assignment reached on the route taken by evaluation:

```
                              empty assignment
                                    |
                            Self.If is true: _
Self.Some ("arg0", _): Lang.QUANT("∃", [X (1, "entity")], _)
                     ["arg0" → [X (1, "entity")]]
                                    |
                            Self.If is false: _
Self.Some ("arg1", _): Lang.QUANT("∃", [X (2, "entity")], _)
                     ["arg0" → [X (1, "entity")]]
                     ["arg1" → [X (2, "entity")]]
                                    |
Self.Some ("event", _): Lang.QUANT("∃", [X (3, "event")], _)
                     ["arg0" → [X (1, "entity")]]
                     ["event" → [X (3, "event")]]
                     ["arg1" → [X (2, "entity")]]
                                    |
                            Self.If is false: _
                            Self.If is false: _
                Self.Rel ("distims", _): Lang.REL ("distims", _)
            _____|_____
           Self.T "event":            Self.T "arg0":              Self.T "arg1":
Lang.At (X (3, "event"), "event") Lang.At (X (1, "entity"), "arg0") Lang.At (X (2, "entity"), "arg1")
```

Evaluation:

1. starts from the empty assignment,
2. finds the sequence assigned "arg0" is null with the first occurrence of SOMEONE and so creates an "arg0" binding with the addition of Lang.X (1, "entity") to the sequence assigned "arg0" and generation of the quantificational construct Lang.QUANT ("∃", [Lang.X (1, "entity")], _),
3. finds the sequence assigned "arg0" is not null with the second SOMEONE and so creates an "arg1" binding with the addition of Lang.X (2, "entity") and corresponding quantificational construct,
4. creates an "event" binding on entry to verb1 with the addition of Lang.X (3, "event") and corresponding quantificational construct,
5. finds the sequence assigned "arg0" is not null,
6. finds the sequence assigned "arg0" is not null, and finally
7. terminates with a transitive verb form that has "event", "arg0" and "arg1" bound arguments.

2.3.2 Nouns and Noun Phrases

Before considering formal encodings for nouns it is necessary to first create the possibility of noun phrases with restrictions as environments able to host nouns. The idea is that the restriction of a noun phrase should be insulated from the containing clause. This is accomplished with NP, which takes two parameters: x for the binding name that the noun phrase opens in the containing clause, and e to provide the content of the noun phrase restriction.

```
val NP =
fn e => fn x =>
 Self.Names (fn lc =>
  Self.Lam (x, "h",
   Self.Clean (0, diff (lc, ["h"]), "",
    Self.Clean (1, ["h"], "", e)))))
```
A call of NP:

1. repositions the first sequence element assigned x to be the first sequence element assigned "h",
2. shifts all other open bindings of the names taken from the call of Names minus "h" to "" bindings, and
3. shifts all sequence values assigned "h" to "" with the exception of the first value.

Shifting a binding to the empty name "" essentially removes the binding from further consideration to leave only the single "h" binding that it is the purpose of the noun phrase to introduce.

Having arguments with restrictions that bind with a given name is accomplished with PP:

```
val PP =
fn x => fn e1 => fn e2 =>
 Self.Some (x, Self.Rel ("∧", [e1 x, e2]))
```

As with SOMEONE in Sect. 2.3.1, the state of the assignment can determine the binding created by a bare noun phrase:

```
val NP1 =
fn e1 => fn e2 =>
 Self.If (fn g: Lang.t Assign.t => null (g "arg0"),
  PP "arg0" (NP e1) e2,
  PP "arg1" (NP e1) e2)
```

Finally encodings for nouns can be considered, for which the simplest form is a predicate with a bound "h" argument:

```
val noun1 =
fn s =>
 Self.Rel (s, [Self.T "h"])
```

The ingredients introduced in this section are brought together with the analysis of (2) as ex4.

(2) Gostak distims doshes.

```
val ex4 =
( (NP1 (noun1 "gostak"))
  ( (NP1 (noun1 "doshes"))
    (verb1 "distims")))
```

Here is an evaluation of ex4:

```
> SelfToLang.eval (fn _ => nil, ex4);
```
val it =
QUANT ("∃", [X (1, "entity")],
REL ("∧", [REL ("gostak", [At (X (1, "entity"), "h")]),
QUANT ("∃", [X (2, "entity")],
REL ("∧", [REL ("doshes", [At (X (2, "entity"), "h")]),
QUANT ("∃", [X (3, "event")],
REL ("distims", [At (X (3, "event"), "event"), At (X (1, "entity"), "arg0"),
At (X (2, "entity"), "arg1")])])])])])
: Lang.t

The Lang.t expression that is the result of evaluation can be pretty printed as follows:

$\exists x_1 (\text{gostak}(x_1) \wedge \exists x_2 (\text{doshes}(x_2) \wedge \exists e_3 \text{distims}(e_3, x_1, x_2)))$

Such a Davidsonian meaning representation retains grammatical role information with fixed arity positions, e.g., achieved with the Davidsonian.format routine of Sect. 1.3.2.

The evaluation of ex4 can be pictured as follows:

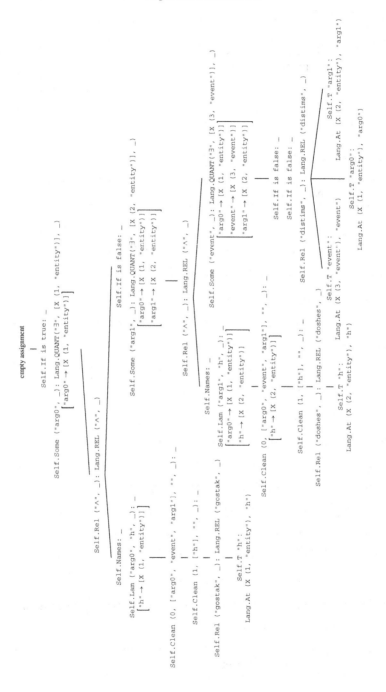

This shows how the binding created by the noun phrase *gostak*, while being opened as an "arg0" binding to bind the subject argument of the main predicate *distims*, shifts to "h" internally to its restriction to bind the nominal *gostak*, and furthermore shifts to " " to have no binding consequence inside the restriction of the subsequent noun phrase containing *doshes*.

The analysis of ex4 discriminates overtly between nouns (with noun1) and verbs (with verb1), but consider word1 which tests for the absence of an "h" binding such that with success a verb encoding is selected while failure selects a noun encoding.

```
val word1 =
fn s =>
 Self.If (fn g: Lang.t Assign.t => null (g "h"),
  verb1 s, noun1 s)
```

With word1 (2) can be analysed as ex5.

```
val ex5 =
( (NP1 (word1 "gostak"))
  ( (NP1 (word1 "doshes"))
    (word1 "distims")))
```

Evaluation of ex5 produces the same result as with the evaluation of ex4.

2.3.3 Adding Non Core Arguments

Examples considered so far had arguments with the privileged grammatical status of creating either "arg0", "arg1" or "h" bindings. Such limited data was covered with encodings that hard wired acceptable combinations of "arg0", "arg1" and "h" bindings. This is obviously inadequate as soon as the presence of other types of argument noun phrases are considered, as are created with preposition phrases in English, such as with *as*, *following*, *including*, *on*, but also more productively *according to*, *compared with*, *out into*, *primarily because of*, and so on. This section offers a method to incorporate such binding names.

Consider recursive addArgs.

```
val rec addArgs =
fn l1 => fn l2 => fn pred =>
 case l1 of
   nil => pred l2
 | x::r =>
     Self.If (fn g: Lang.t Assign.t => null (g x),
       addArgs r l2 pred,
       addArgs r (l2 @ [x]) pred)
```

This takes three parameters: l1 and l2 as sequences of binding names and pred that will itself have an open parameter to take a sequence of binding names. When l1 is `nil` the content of `12` is applied to `pred`, otherwise an expression is created with `Self.If` that has:

1. a test for whether the first element of `11` is assigned the empty sequence,
2. an expression to evaluate if the test succeeds assembled from a call to `addArgs` on the rest of `11` with no change to `12`, and
3. an expression to evaluate if the test fails assembled from a call to `addArgs` on the rest of `11` with `12` extended to include the first element of `11`.

Predicates can be created with `predicate`, which calls `addArgs` as a wrapper around `Self.Rel` that creates at the very least arguments for the names of `args`, and possibly other arguments built from names taken from the call of `Self.Names` minus the names of `args` such that these added arguments will only have consequences when there is sufficient binding support from the assignment during evaluation.

```
val predicate =
fn args => fn s =>
 Self.Names (fn lc =>
  addArgs (diff (lc, args)) args (
   fn l => Self.Rel (s, map (fn x => Self.T x) l)))
```

Encodings for nouns and verbs can now be created.

```
val noun =
fn s =>
 predicate ["h"] s

val verb =
fn s => fn args =>
 Self.Some ("event", predicate (["event"] @ args) s)
```

These differ in that the ever present argument for verbs is a locally created `"event"` rather than an inherited `"h"` binding. Also `verb` has an extra parameter `args` for taking a sequence of binding names that have to be arguments of the verb.

A generic coding for words, with sensitivity to the presence of an `"h"` binding, can be offered:

```
val word =
fn s =>
 Self.If (fn g: Lang.t Assign.t => null (g "h"),
  verb s nil,
  noun s)
```

The PP operation of Sect. 2.3.2 already gives a method to create arguments that bind with non-core binding names. Also, NP2 can be made to provide genitive bindings in nominal contexts, while otherwise calling the binding actions of NP1.

```
val NP2 =
fn e1 => fn e2 =>
 Self.If (fn g: Lang.t Assign.t => null (g "h"),
  NP1 e1 e2,
  PP "of" (NP e1) e2)
```

The ingredients introduced in this section are brought together with the analysis of (3) as ex6.

(3) For Americans Buffalo gostak distims doshes.

```
val ex6 =
( (PP "for"
      (NP (word "Americans")))
   ( (NP2 ( (NP2 (word "Buffalo"))
            (word "gostak")))
    ( (NP2 (word "doshes"))
     (word "distims"))))
```

Here is an evaluation of ex6:

```
> SelfToLang.eval (fn _ => nil, ex6);
```
val it =
QUANT ("∃", [X (1, "entity")],
 REL ("∧", [REL ("Americans", [At (X (1, "entity"), "h")]),
  QUANT ("∃", [X (2, "entity")],
   REL ("∧", [
   QUANT ("∃", [X (3, "entity")],
    REL ("∧", [REL ("Buffalo", [At (X (3, "entity"), "h")]),
     REL ("gostak", [At (X (2, "entity"), "h"), At (X (3, "entity"), "of")])])),
   QUANT ("∃", [X (4, "entity")],
    REL ("∧", [REL ("doshes", [At (X (4, "entity"), "h")]),
     QUANT ("∃", [X (5, "event")],
      REL ("distims", [At (X (5, "event"), "event"),
      At (X (1, "entity"), "for"), At (X (2, "entity"), "arg0"),
      At (X (4, "entity"), "arg1")])])])])])]))
: Lang.t

This shows creation of "event", "for", "arg0" and "arg1" bindings of the main predicate, *distims*. In addition to the "h" binding for the nominal *gostak* there is also an "of" binding created locally to the *gostak* noun phrase which is restricted by binding *Buffalo* under the "h" name. Pretty printing returns:

$\exists x_1$ (Americans (x_1) ∧
 $\exists x_2$ ($\exists x_3$ (Buffalo (x_3) ∧ is_gostak_of (x_2, x_3)) ∧
  $\exists x_4$ (doshes (x_4) ∧ $\exists e_5$ (distims (e_5, x_2, x_4) ∧ for (e_5) = x_1))))

The pretty print involves fixing grammatical roles to arity positions. But this is not possible with the "for" binding of the main predicate, and so there is integration of this adjunct binding as a modifier of the event (e_5) of the main predicate. This is achieved with `Davidsonian.format` of Sect. 1.3.2. `Davidsonian.format` is also responsible for changing the nominal *gostak* predicate to accommodate the genitive binding.

2.4 Summary

This chapter introduced conditional `Self.If` as part of the `'a Self.t` language, and included a Standard ML implementation of a recursive routine for evaluating `Lang.t` `Self.t` expressions against a sequence assignment function that stores accumulated binding information to return expressions of `Lang.t`. Having `Self.If` enabled an automated selection of expression content at the runtime of evaluation based on the state of the assignment function. This (i) allowed for single encodings of content that would otherwise require distinct expressions, and (ii) equipped expressions with ways to recover from situations that would otherwise lead to unwelcome results from evaluation. With these two properties evaluation was left to feed automatic regulation to enable coverage of unknown lexical items as well as novel binding names. This is especially notable for providing a means to get away with very little explicit coding of information about how binding dependencies should be established.

References

Berkling KJ (1976) A symmetric complement to the lambda-calculus. Interner Bericht ISF-76-7, GMD. St. Augustin, Germany

Butler A (2007) Scope control and grammatical dependencies. J Log Lang Inf 16:241–264

Butler A (2010) The semantics of grammatical dependencies. Current research in the semantics/pragmatics interface, vol 23. Emerald, Bingley

Dekker P (2002) Meaning and use of indefinite expressions. J Log Lang Inf 11:141–194

Dekker P (2012) Dynamic semantics. Studies in linguistics and philosophy, vol 91. Springer, Dordrecht

Hendriks D, van Oostrom V (2003) Adbmal-calculus. Department of Philosophy, Utrecht University

Hollenberg M, Vermeulen CFM (1996) Counting variables in a dynamic setting. J Log Comput 6:725–744

Richards IA, Ogden CK (1923) The meaning of meaning. A Harvest Book/Harcourt, Brace & World Inc, New York

van Eijck J (2001) Incremental dynamics. J Log Lang Inf 10:319–351

Vermeulen CFM (1993) Sequence semantics for dynamic predicate logic. J Log Lang Inf 2:217–254

Vermeulen CFM (2000) Variables as stacks: a case study in dynamic model theory. J Log Lang Inf 9:143–167

Visser A, Vermeulen CFM (1996) Dynamic bracketing and discourse representation. Notre Dame J Form Log 37:321–365

Chapter 3
Self-Locating Evaluation

In the previous chapter sequence assignment state allowed selecting between different evaluations of words. The idea of utilising the assignment as a source of information about the content of the expression under evaluation is developed further in this chapter, with sequence assignments employed to determine where dependencies are located throughout an evaluation. This is achieved with a new language, Scope Control Theory or SCT, that includes fine grained and often inter dependent primitive operations of scope manipulation. In particular binding can require multiple distinct operations (see below Sct.Close occurring with Sct.Use and Sct.Lam for creating bindings, while Sct.Rel governs the release and subsequent accessibility of bindings following counts of Sct.Use). The method is shown to be flexible but constrained to support processing structures close to expected conventional parsings of natural language, so much so that a link with existing parsed annotations will be established in Chap. 4.

The chapter proceeds as follows. Section 3.1 introduces the SCT language, as well as Sct.count and Sct.collect for extracting information from SCT expressions, and Sct.manage for organising the distribution of binding information in sequence assignments. Section 3.2 provides an evaluation routine for reaching expressions of the Lang.t language of Sect. 1.3. Section 3.3 gives links with natural language by encoding grammatical roles, arguments and predicates. Section 3.4 is a summary.

3.1 Scope Control Theory

The 'a Sct.t datatype defines the SCT language.

```
structure Sct =
struct
datatype 'a t =
   Use of string * 'a t
 | CUse of 'a * string * 'a t
```

© Springer International Publishing Switzerland 2015
A. Butler, *Linguistic Expressions and Semantic Processing*,
DOI 10.1007/978-3-319-18830-0_3

```
  | Hide of string * 'a t
  | There of string * 'a t
  | T of string * int
  | At of 'a t * string
  | Close of string * (string * string) * string list * 'a t
  | CClose of string * 'a t
  | Rel of string list * string list * string * 'a t list
  | If of ('a Assign.t -> bool) * 'a t * 'a t
  | Lam of string * string * 'a t
  | Copy of string * string * 'a t
  | Clean of int * string list * string * 'a t
  | QuantThrow of (string * string) * 'a t
  | Throw of string * 'a t
  | Pick of string * 'a t * ('a list -> 'a list) * string list

fun count (x: string, f: 'a t): int =
 case f of
   Use (y, e) =>
    if x = y then count (x, e) + 1 else count (x, e)
  | CUse (_, y, e) =>
    if x = y then count (x, e) + 1 else count (x, e)
  | Hide (y, e) => if x = y then 0 else count (x, e)
  | There (y, e) =>
    let
     val c = count (x, e)
    in
     if x = y andalso c > 0 then c - 1 else c
    end
  | T _ => 0
  | At (e, _) => count (x, e)
  | Close (_, _, _, e) => count (x, e)
  | CClose (_, e) => count (x, e)
  | Rel (_, _, _, es) => sumcount (x, es)
  | If (_, e, _) => count (x, e)
  | Lam (_, _, e) => count (x, e)
  | Copy (_, _, e) => count (x, e)
  | Clean (_, _, _, e) => count (x, e)
  | QuantThrow (_, e) => count (x, e)
  | Throw (_, e) => count (x, e)
  | Pick _ => 0
and sumcount (x: string, es: 'a t list): int =
 foldr (fn (e, n) => count (x, e) + n) 0 es

fun collect (x: string, f: 'a t): 'a list =
 case f of
   Use (_, e) => collect (x, e)
```

```
  | CUse (v, y, e) =>
     if x = y then [v] @ collect (x, e) else collect (x, e)
  | Hide (y, e) => if x = y then nil else collect (x, e)
  | There (_, e) => collect (x, e)
  | T _ => nil
  | At (e, _) => collect (x, e)
  | Close (_, _, _, e) => collect (x, e)
  | CClose (_, e) => collect (x, e)
  | Rel (_, _, _, es) =>
     foldr (fn (e, l) => l @ collect (x, e)) nil es
  | If (_, e, _) => collect (x, e)
  | Lam (_, _, e) => collect (x, e)
  | Copy (_, _, e) => collect (x, e)
  | Clean (_, _, _, e) => collect (x, e)
  | QuantThrow (_, e) => collect (x, e)
  | Throw (_, e) => collect (x, e)
  | Pick _ => nil
fun allocate (x: string, y: string, n: int, es: 'a t list,
      g: 'a Assign.t): 'a Assign.t =
  let
   val a = sumcount (x, List.drop (es, n+1))
   val b = sumcount (x, List.take (es, n))
  in
   iterate
    (Assign.shiftLast x y)
    b
    (iterate (fn h => Assign.pop (x, h)) a g)
  end

fun manage (xs: string list, ys: string list,
      n: int, es: 'a t list, g: 'a Assign.t): 'a Assign.t =
  case xs of
    nil => g
  | x::rxs =>
      case ys of
        nil => raise Empty
      | y::rys =>
          manage (rxs, rys, n, es, allocate (x, y, n, es, g))
end
```

The combined purpose of Sct.Use, Sct.CUse, Sct.Hide and Sct.There is to signal the distributions of bindings for the expression of which they are part. A handle on this contribution is gained with Sct.count (x, f) that takes a string x and expression f and returns the number of occurrences within f of Sct.Use (x, _) or Sct.CUse (x, _) outside the scope of any Sct.Hide (x, _). Furthermore Sct.There (x, _) will decrement a positive count. Here are examples of Sct.count obtaining counts for the "ENTITY" name:

```
> Sct.count ("ENTITY",
    Sct.Use ("ENTITY",
      Sct.Hide ("ENTITY",
        Sct.Use ("ENTITY", Sct.Rel (nil, nil, "", nil)))));
val it = 1: int

> Sct.count ("ENTITY",
    Sct.Use ("ENTITY",
      Sct.There ("ENTITY",
        Sct.Use ("ENTITY", Sct.Rel (nil, nil, "", nil)))));
val it = 1: int

> Sct.count ("ENTITY",
    Sct.Use ("ENTITY",
      Sct.Use ("ENTITY",
        Sct.There ("ENTITY", Sct.Rel (nil, nil, "", nil)))));
val it = 2: int
```

Function Sct.sumcount (x, es) returns the sum of all counts for x in expressions of es. For example:

```
> Sct.sumcount ("ENTITY", [
    Sct.Use ("ENTITY", Sct.Rel (nil, nil, "", nil)),
    Sct.Rel (nil, nil, "", nil),
    Sct.Use ("ENTITY", Sct.Rel (nil, nil, "", nil))]);
val it = 2: int
```

Function Sct.collect of type string * 'a Sct.t -> 'a list gathers 'a values carried by instances of Sct.CUse. For example:

```
> Sct.collect ("constant",
    Sct.CUse (1, "constant",
      Sct.CUse (2, "constant", Sct.Rel (nil, nil, "", nil))));
val it = [1, 2]: int list
```

An x collection will terminate with Sct.Hide (x, _). For example:

```
> Sct.collect ("constant",
    Sct.CUse (1, "constant",
      Sct.Hide ("constant",
        Sct.CUse (2, "constant", Sct.Rel (nil, nil, "", nil)))));
val it = [1]: int list
```

Function Sct.allocate (x, y, n, es, g) modifies assignment g by removing with Assign.pop the first a elements of the sequence assigned x and repositioning with Assign.shiftLast the last b elements of the sequence assigned x to become the first b elements of the sequence assigned y. The values of a and b are dependent on two additional parameters, integer n and list of 'a Sct.t expressions es, where:

$$a = \sum_{i=n+1}^{length(es)-1} \texttt{Sct.count (x, List.nth (es, i))}$$

$$b = \sum_{i=0}^{n-1} \texttt{Sct.count (x, List.nth (es, i))}$$

The motivation for these values of a and b is the desire to allocate the correct sequence values assigned x with respect to the nth expression of es following the expectation of *expression integrity*, namely that:

$$\texttt{length (g x)} = \sum_{i=0}^{length(es)-1} \texttt{Sct.count (x, List.nth (es, i))}$$

That is, the length of the sequence assigned x by g should match the sum of counts for x in the expressions of es. Under expression integrity a is the total usage count of expressions that are subsequent to the nth expression of es and b is that of prior expressions. For a particular expression of es, i.e. for a particular value of n, changes brought about to the assignment involve removing (with Assign.pop) a values of the sequence assigned to x that are intended for subsequent expressions, and reallocating (with Assign.shiftLast) b values that are present to satisfy the use counts of prior expressions. This removes those x bindings that support subsequent expressions, while leaving accessible those x bindings that support prior expressions, only under the y binding name. After the iterations of Assign.pop and Assign.shiftLast, the number of sequence values remaining assigned to x will be length (g x) - a - b = Sct.count (x, List.nth(es, n)), that is, the correct number required to support the nth expression of es.

   With recursive function Sct.manage (xs, ys, n, es, g) the content of xs and ys provides x and y values for applications of Sct.allocate (x, y, n, es, g) to modify assignment g. List ys should be at least as long as xs to avoid the Empty exception. For example:

```
> val g: int Assign.t = fn "ENTITY" => [2, 1] | _ => nil;
val g = fn: int Assign.t

> val xs = ["ENTITY"];
val xs = ["ENTITY"]: string list

> val ys = ["c"];
val ys = ["c"]: string list

> val es: int Sct.t list = [
   Sct.Use ("ENTITY", Sct.Rel (nil, nil, "", nil)),
   Sct.Rel (nil, nil, "", nil),
   Sct.Use ("ENTITY", Sct.Rel (nil, nil, "", nil))];
```

val es =
  [Use ("ENTITY", Rel ([], [], "", [])), Rel ([], [], "", []),
  Use ("ENTITY", Rel ([], [], "", []))]: int Sct.t list

```
> val g0 = Sct.manage (xs, ys, 0, es, g);
```
val g0 = fn: int Assign.t

```
> val g1 = Sct.manage (xs, ys, 1, es, g);
```
val g1 = fn: int Assign.t

```
> val g2 = Sct.manage (xs, ys, 2, es, g);
```
val g2 = fn: int Assign.t

```
> g0 "ENTITY";
```
val it = [1]: int list

```
> g1 "ENTITY";
```
val it = []: int list

```
> g2 "ENTITY";
```
val it = [2]: int list

```
> g0 "c";
```
val it = []: int list

```
> g1 "c";
```
val it = [1]: int list

```
> g2 "c";
```
val it = [1]: int list

3.2 Evaluation

Following the approach taken to investigate the `'a Self.t` language in Chap. 2, the SCT language will be explored with an evaluation routine, `SctToLang.eval`. Being relativised against `Lang.t Assign.t` assignments, `SctToLang.eval` will transform `Lang.t Sct.t` expressions into `Lang.t` expressions. In transforming to `Lang.t` expressions, to ensure the Barendregt variable convention (see Sect. 1.1.3) is obeyed by the resulting `Lang.t` expression, variables of the `Lang.t` language should be fresh when added to assigned sequences. This is assured with reference to `SctToLang.cnt` that has a starting state of 0.

```
structure SctToLang =
struct

val cnt = ref 0;
```

```
fun env (l: (string * string) list, g: Lang.t Assign.t):
Lang.t Assign.t =
 foldr (fn ((x, sort), h) =>
  (inc cnt ; Assign.push (Lang.X (!cnt, sort), x, h))) g l

fun eval (g: Lang.t Assign.t, f: Lang.t Sct.t): Lang.t =
 case f of
    Sct.Use (_, e) => eval (g, e)
  | Sct.CUse (_, _, e) => eval (g, e)
  | Sct.Hide (_, e) => eval (g, e)
  | Sct.There (_, e) => eval (g, e)
  | Sct.T (x, n) =>
    hd ((iterate (fn h => Assign.pop (x, h)) n g) x)
  | Sct.At (e, s) => Lang.At (eval (g, e), s)
  | Sct.Close (oper, (x, sort), xs, e) =>
    let
      val c = Sct.count (x, e)
      val h = env (List.tabulate (c, fn _ => (x, sort)), g)
    in
      Lang.Quant (x, xs, oper,
       List.tabulate (c, fn i => eval (h, Sct.T (x, i))),
        eval (h, e))
    end
  | Sct.CClose (x, e) =>
    eval (
      foldr (fn (y, h) =>
       Assign.push (y, x, h)) g (Sct.collect (x, e)), e)
  | Sct.Rel (xs, ys, s, es) =>
    Lang.REL (s, List.tabulate (length es, fn n =>
     eval (Sct.manage (xs, ys, n, es, g), List.nth (es, n))))
  | Sct.If (func, e1, e2) =>
    if func g then eval (g, e1) else eval (g, e2)
  | Sct.Lam (x, y, e) =>
    eval (Assign.pop (x, Assign.push (hd (g x), y, g)), e)
  | Sct.Copy (x, y, e) =>
    eval (Assign.push (hd (g x), y, g), e)
  | Sct.Clean (n, xs, y, e) =>
    eval (Assign.manage (n, xs, y, g), e)
  | Sct.QuantThrow ((x, sort), e) =>
    let
      val h = env ([(x, sort)], g)
    in
      Lang.QuantThrow (x, eval (h, Sct.T (x, 0)), eval (h, e))
    end
  | Sct.Throw (x, e) => Lang.Throw (x, eval (g, e))
```

```
| Sct.Pick (s, e, func, xs) =>
    Lang.REL
      (s ^ ":pick", [eval (g, e)] @ func (List.concat (map g xs)))

end
```

Content is added to an existing assignment with SctToLang.env. This takes a list of paired strings, with the first string a binding name that is to be assigned a fresh first value, where a value is a Lang.x expression with sort information taken from the second string of the pair. For example, the following illustrates introduction to the empty assignment of two sequence values to be assigned to the "situation" binding name, both of sort "situation"; and one sequence value for the "ENTITY" binding name of sort "entity":

```
> val g = SctToLang.env (
    [("ENTITY", "entity"),
     ("situation", "situation"),
     ("situation", "situation")], fn _ => nil);
val g = fn: string -> Lang.t Assign.t

> g "situation";
val it = [X (2, "situation"), X (1, "situation")]: Lang.t list

> g "ENTITY";
val it = [X (3, "entity")]: Lang.t list
```

Sct.Use, Sct.CUse, Sct.Hide and Sct.There have no impact once reached during an evaluation, other than returning the evaluation of the embedded expression. Rather consequences arise when Sct.count or Sct.collect are invoked (see Sect. 3.1).

Sct.T (x, i) returns the ith value of the sequence assigned x. If there is no ith value an exception is raised. For example:

```
> SctToLang.eval (
    fn "arg0" => [Lang.X (2, "entity"), Lang.X (1, "entity")]
     | _ => nil,
    Sct.T ("arg0", 0));
val it = X (2, "entity"): Lang.t

> SctToLang.eval (
    fn "arg0" => [Lang.X (2, "entity"), Lang.X (1, "entity")]
     | _ => nil,
    Sct.T ("arg0", 1));
val it = X (1, "entity"): Lang.t

> SctToLang.eval (
    fn "arg0" => [Lang.X (2, "entity"), Lang.X (1, "entity")]
     | _ => nil,
```

```
    Sct.T ("arg0", 2));
```
Exception- Empty raised

Evaluation of Sct.At (e, s) returns a role value construct with Lang.At taking the evaluation of e as expression content, and the name s to indicate grammatical role (for more about role value constructs, see Sect. 1.3.1). For example:

```
> SctToLang.eval (
    fn "arg0" => [Lang.X (2, "entity")]
     | _ => nil,
    Sct.At (Sct.T ("arg0", 0), "arg0"));
```
val it = At (X (2, "entity"), "arg0"): Lang.t

```
> SctToLang.eval (
    fn _ => nil,
    Sct.At (Sct.Rel (nil, nil, "", nil), "that"));
```
val it = At (REL ("", []), "that"): Lang.t

In the 'a Self.t language of Chap. 2, role value constructs occurred only at the terminal level. With Sct.At being independent, role value constructs can occur at any level of structure, a flexibility that assists considering clausal embeddings from Sect. 3.3.8 onwards.

Sct.Close (oper, (x, sort), xs, e) adds Sct.count (x, e) new values with the sort information of sort to the sequence assigned x and returns Lang.Quant for oper to bind as variables the newly introduced values and scope over the evaluation of e against the adjusted assignment. The returned Lang.Quant is also given hooks (see Sect. 1.3.1) to capture thrown x bindings, as well as thrown restriction materials for the binding names listed in xs, of which x is typically a member. For example:

```
> SctToLang.eval (
    fn _ => nil,
    Sct.Close ("∃", ("ENTITY", "entity"), ["ENTITY"],
     Sct.Use ("ENTITY", Sct.Rel (nil, nil, "", nil))));
```
val it =
Quant ("ENTITY", ["ENTITY"], "∃", [X (1, "entity")], REL ("", []))
: Lang.t

What occurs can be pictured as follows:

```
                             empty assignment
                                   |
Sct.Close ("∃","ENTITY", ["ENTITY"], _): Lang.Quant("ENTITY", ["ENTITY"], "∃", [X (1, "entity")], _)
                       ["ENTITY" → [X (1, "entity")]]
                                   |
                        Sct.Use ("ENTITY", _): _
                 Sct.Rel ([], [], "", nil): Lang.REL ("", [])
```

Beginning from the empty assignment, a fresh value `Lang.X (1, "entity")` is entered as a value of the sequence assigned `"ENTITY"`.

`Sct.Close` can be triggered to create multiple fresh bindings:

```
> SctToLang.eval (
    fn _ => nil,
    Sct.Close ("∃", ("ENTITY", "entity"), ["ENTITY"],
     Sct.Use ("ENTITY",
      Sct.Use ("ENTITY", Sct.Rel (nil, nil, "", nil)))))) ;
```
val it =
Quant ("ENTITY", ["ENTITY"], "∃", [X (2, "entity"), X (1, "entity")], REL ("", []))
: Lang.t

An `Sct.Close` instance might create no fresh bindings, but will still bring about hooks to capture thrown material:

```
> SctToLang.eval (
    fn _ => nil,
    Sct.Close ("∃", ("ENTITY", "entity"), ["ENTITY"],
     Sct.Hide ("ENTITY",
      Sct.Use ("ENTITY", Sct.Rel (nil, nil, "", nil)))))) ;
```
val it =
Quant ("ENTITY", ["ENTITY"], "∃", [], REL ("", []))
: Lang.t

`Sct.CClose (x, e)` invokes `Sct.collect` to return values that are introduced into the assignment as new sequence values assigned `x`.

`Sct.Rel (xs, ys, s, es)` returns a relation s that has the evaluation of the nth expression of es as the nth argument. With evaluation of the entire relation against sequence assignment `g`, the nth expression of es is evaluated against the possibly different assignment `Sct.manage (xs, ys, n, es, g)`. For example suppose:

```
val ex1 =
Sct.Rel (["ENTITY"], ["c"], "", [
 Sct.Use ("ENTITY", Sct.Rel (nil, nil, "", nil)),
 Sct.Rel (nil, nil, "", nil),
 Sct.Use ("ENTITY", Sct.Rel (nil, nil, "", nil))])
```

then:

```
> SctToLang.eval (
    fn "ENTITY" => [Lang.X (2, "entity"), Lang.X (1, "entity")]
     | _ => nil,
    ex1) ;
```
val it =
REL ("", [REL ("", []), REL ("", []), REL ("", [])])
: Lang.t

It is what happens during the evaluation that is of interest, which can be pictured as follows:

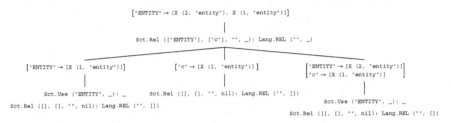

An argument of Sct.Rel (["ENTITY"], ["c"], "", _) that brings about support for an "ENTITY" binding with Sct.Use ("ENTITY", _), in addition to ensuring an "ENTITY" binding for the argument, brings about the effect of transferring the supported binding to a "c" binding for subsequent arguments. But the reverse is impossible: an "ENTITY" binding supported by a subsequent argument is made totally absent from the bindings available for prior arguments.

Like Self.If introduced in Sect.2.2, Sct.If (func, e1, e2) takes Lang.t Assign.t -> bool function func to test the current assignment state such that the evaluation continues with e1 when the test is true, while otherwise continuing with e2.

Following Self.Lam introduced in Sect.2.2, Sct.Lam (x, y, e) returns the evaluation of e against an assignment state where what had been the first element of the sequence assigned x is repositioned to be the first element of the sequence assigned y.

Sct.Copy (x, y, e) returns the evaluation of e against assignment g modified with Assign.push (hd (g x), y, g). For example suppose:

```
val ex2 =
Sct.Copy ("event", "fact",
 Sct.Rel (nil, nil, "", [
  Sct.T ("event", 0), Sct.T ("fact", 0)])))
```

then

```
> SctToLang.eval (
   fn "event" => [Lang.X (1, "event")]
    | _ => nil,
   ex2);
```
val it = REL ("", [X (1, "event"), X (1, "event")]): Lang.t

What occurs can be pictured as follows:

```
["event" → [X (1, "event")]]
                    |
       Sct.Copy ("event","fact", _):  _
       ⎡"event" → [X (1, "event")]⎤
       ⎣"fact"  → [X (1, "event")]⎦
                    |
   Sct.Rel ([], [], "", _): Lang.REL ("", _)
```

Sct.T ("event", 0): X (1, "event")   Sct.T ("fact", 0): X (1, "event")

That is, evaluation of Sct.Rel (nil, nil, "", [Sct.T ("event", 0), Sct.T ("fact", 0)]) takes place against an assignment state where the first element of the sequence assigned "event" is copied to also be the first element of the sequence assigned "fact".

Like Self.Clean introduced in Sect. 2.2, Sct.Clean (n, xs, y, e) modifies the assignment g with Assign.manage (n, xs, y, g), and returns the evaluation of e against the altered assignment.

Sct.QuantThrow ((x, sort), e) adds a means to create a single fresh x binding with the sort information sort. A binding so introduced can only have consequences for the content of e but might, following post-processing, receive a wider scope positioning, as will be demonstrated in Sect. 3.3.1.

Sct.Throw (x, e) offers a method to relocate expression material, as illustrated in Sect. 3.3.3.

Sct.Pick (s, e, func, xs) provides a way for an expression e to be related by s to sequence values assigned to the names of xs that are selected with func. This is employed to gather accessible antecedents for pronouns in Sect. 3.3.6.

3.3 Grammatical Roles, Arguments and Predicates

A binding name has a grammatical role when either:

1. it can be the name x of a bound term Sct.T (x, 0) that serves as a predicate argument, henceforth referred to as a *local binding*;
2. it will not bind terms but during an evaluation may harbour values that shift to local binding names, referred to as a *fresh binding*; or
3. it will not bind terms that are predicate arguments but during an evaluation may harbour values that shift from local binding names, referred to as a *context binding*.

Names with differing roles are always to be kept distinct. This is achieved by declaring a list lc of the possible local binding names, and a list fh of the possible fresh binding names, while any other name has potential of taking on a context binding role.

Control over the release of values as either fresh bindings or context bindings is typically achieved with manage. Parameter fh takes a list of fresh binding names, while all values for context bindings are collected as sequence values assigned to the privileged "c" name.

```
val manage =
fn fh => fn es =>
 Sct.Rel (fh, map (fn _ => "c") fh, "", es)
```

The remainder of this section proceeds as follows. Section 3.3.1 begins the discussion of arguments with what is the simplest method of argument creation. Section 3.3.2 details the coding of predicates with bound arguments. To argument introduction, Sect. 3.3.3 adds noun phrase restrictions. Section 3.3.4 considers bringing about fresh bindings with closures for providing the new values adopted by arguments. Section 3.3.5 extends argument coverage to include proper names. Section 3.3.6 details pronouns. Section 3.3.7 contributes quantification that packages closures with argument forming operations. Section 3.3.8 extends coverage of predicates to include verbs with finite clause embeddings. Section 3.3.9 covers examples of control with verbs that embed infinitive clauses. Finally, Sect. 3.3.10 demonstrates nouns with clause embedding.

3.3.1 Classic Arguments

The purpose of an argument is to introduce a local binding. One way to create a local binding is with classic. This takes pair of strings (v, sort), with v a fresh binding name that is assigned a newly created first value that is a Lang.x expression with sort information from sort. Additionally there are x and e parameters, such that the binding created for v is repositioned to form a value assigned to the local binding name x before evaluation of e. Being created with Sct.QuantThrow, the fresh binding will take with post-processing (see Sect. 1.3.1) the scope position of the first commanding Lang.Quant (v, _, _, _). Also, with clean, before there is creation and shifting to x of a binding, any sequence value assigned x is relocated to the "c" context binding name with Sct.Clean.

```
val clean =
fn x => fn e =>
 Sct.Clean (0, [x], "c", e)

val classic =
fn (v, sort) => fn x => fn e =>
 clean x (
   Sct.QuantThrow ((v, sort), Sct.Lam (v, x, e)))
```

The following illustrates an evaluation of classic that is embedded under Lang.t expression material, such that after post-processing with Post.transform (see

Sect. 1.3.1) the quantification of the derived Lang.QuantThrow scopes with the commanding "ENTITY" closure of Lang.Quant.

```
> Lang.Quant ("ENTITY", ["ENTITY"], "∃", nil,
    Lang.REL ("¬", [
      SctToLang.eval (
        fn _ => nil,
        classic ("ENTITY", "entity") "x" (Sct.T ("x", 0)))]));
```
val it =
Quant ("ENTITY", ["ENTITY"], "∃", [],
REL ("¬", [QuantThrow ("ENTITY", X (1, "entity"), X (1, "entity"))]))
: Lang.t

```
> Post.transform it;
```
val it =
QUANT ("∃", [X (1, "entity")], REL ("¬", [X (1, "entity")]))
: Lang.t

3.3.2 Predicates

This section details the coding of predicates. However discussion of predicates that take clausal embeddings is deferred until Sect. 3.3.8. Basic predicate relations are created with rel:

```
val rel =
fn s => fn es =>
 Sct.Rel (nil, nil, s, es)
```

With the empty list instances, there is no manipulation by Sct.Rel of the assignment g during evaluation, so that each expression of es is evaluated against g, exactly as was the case with Self.Rel in Sect. 2.2.

Having evaluation self-determine missing argument information is achieved with the addArgs function of Sect. 2.3.3, adjusted to take the Sct.If operation:

```
val rec addArgs =
fn l1 => fn l2 => fn pred =>
 case l1 of
   nil => pred l2
 | x::r =>
     Sct.If (fn g: Lang.t Assign.t => null (g x),
       addArgs r l2 pred,
       addArgs r (l2 @ [x]) pred)
```

A call of addArgs gives the basis for constructing arguments for pred which are only evaluated when the state of the evaluation contains binding support from the assignment.

Building on rel and addArgs, predicate defines a general method to form predicates. This allows for bound arguments constructed from the local binding names given with the lc parameter that are additional to required bound arguments constructed from the names of the args parameter. Parameter extra leaves open further extending the arguments taken by the predicate. Parameter s receives the predicate name.

```
val predicate =
fn lc => fn args => fn extra => fn s =>
 addArgs (diff (lc, args)) args (
  fn l => rel s (
   (map (fn x => Sct.At (Sct.T (x, 0), x)) l) @ extra))
```

Bound arguments constructed with predicate have internal structure with Sct.At containing both a bound term and a string name to provide information about the grammatical role of the bound argument, where the given string is the binding name of the bound term. Following Sect. 1.3.2, having such internal structure has consequences for post-processing the output from evaluation to achieve a Davidsonian format.

To create encodings for nouns nn calls predicate requiring at least a "h" binding.

```
val nn =
fn lc => fn s =>
 predicate lc ["h"] nil s
```

Here is a demonstration of nn:

```
val ex3 = nn ["h", "in"] "lawyer"
```

Executing ex3 at the Standard ML prompt results in the following reduced Lang.t Sct.t expression:

```
> ex3;
val ex3 =
If (fn, Rel ([], [], "lawyer", [At (T ("h", 0), "h")]),
 Rel ([], [], "lawyer", [At (T ("h", 0), "h"), At (T ("in", 0), "in")]))
: Sct.t
```

An example of a successful evaluation is as follows:

```
> SctToLang.eval (
   fn "h" => [Lang.X (2, "entity")]
    | "in" => [Lang.X (1, "entity")]
    | _ => nil,
   ex3);
val it =
```

REL ("lawyer", [At (X (2, "entity"), "h"), At (X (1, "entity"), "in")])
: Lang.t

The state of the assignment with its single `"h"` and `"in"` bindings forces an evaluation of the second expression of the `Sct.If` condition which has arguments taking `"h"` and `"in"` bindings:

```
┌ "h"  → [X (2, "entity")] ┐
└ "in" → [X (1, "entity")] ┘

              │

        Sct.If is false: _

Sct.Rel ([], [], "lawyer", _): Lang.REL ("lawyer", _)
   _____/_____

Sct.At (_, "h"): Lang.At (_, "h")        Sct.At (_, "in"): Lang.At (_, "in")

Sct.T ("h", 0): X (2, "entity")          Sct.T ("in", 0): X (1, "entity")
```

Also consider evaluation with an assignment that contains only a single `"h"` binding:

```
> SctToLang.eval (
    fn "h" => [Lang.X (1, "entity")]
     | _ => nil,
    ex3);
```
val it =
REL ("lawyer", [At (X (1, "entity"), "h")])
: Lang.t

The assignment state forces an evaluation of the first expression of the `Sct.If` condition which has only the compulsory argument of a noun that takes an `"h"` binding.

```
[ "h" → [X (1, "entity")] ]

           │

      Sct.If is true: _

Sct.Rel ([], [], "lawyer", _): Lang.REL ("lawyer", _)

           │

  Sct.At (_, "h"): Lang.At (_, "h")

  Sct.T ("h", 0): X (1, "entity")
```

3.3.3 Noun Phrases

Noun phrases should insulate any restriction from the containing clause by shifting open local bindings to a contextual binding name with the exception of the binding introduced by the noun phrase, which should shift to an "h" binding to be available for the restriction content. Such insulation is accomplished with NP introduced in Sect. 2.3.2, but now adjusted to send open local non-"h" bindings to "c", as well as take parameters lc and keep.

```
val NP =
fn keep => fn lc => fn e => fn x =>
 Sct.Lam (x, "h",
  Sct.Clean (0, diff (lc, keep @ ["h"]), "c",
   Sct.Clean (1, ["h"], "", e)))
```

A call of NP:

1. turns the x binding into an "h" binding,
2. shifts to "c" all other open bindings of the names in lc minus the names of keep and "h", and
3. shifts to "" all values of the sequence assigned "h" with the exception of the frontmost sequence value.

The empty name "" binding serves to remove bindings from further consideration.

Now consider someClassic which creates a fresh argument binding with noun phrase restriction support. Being created with classic, the scope of a new binding will differ after post-processing from its location at evaluation. To ensure restriction material accompanies the quantification introduction, Sct.Throw (v, _) surrounds the restriction, sharing the same binding name (v) used to create the new argument binding.

```
val someClassic =
fn lc => fn fh => fn (v, sort) => fn keep =>
fn e1 => fn x => fn e2 =>
 classic (v, sort) x (
  manage fh [Sct.Throw (v, NP keep lc e1 x), e2])
```

The following illustrates evaluation of someClassic embedded under Lang.t expression material.

```
> Lang.Quant ("ENTITY", ["ENTITY"], "∃", nil,
   Lang.REL ("¬", [
    SctToLang.eval (
     fn _ => nil,
     someClassic
      ["h", "arg0"] ["ENTITY"] ("ENTITY", "entity") nil
      (nn ["h", "arg0"] "boy") "arg0" (Sct.T ("arg0", 0)))])]);
```

val it =
Quant ("ENTITY", ["ENTITY"], "∃", [],
REL ("¬", [
 QuantThrow ("ENTITY", X (1, "entity"),
  REL ("", [Throw ("ENTITY", REL ("boy", [At (X (1, "entity"), "h")]))),
   X (1, "entity")]))]))
: Lang.t

Post-processing with `Post.transform` yields:

```
> Post.transform it;
```
val it =
QUANT ("∃", [X (1, "entity")],
 REL ("∧", [REL ("boy", [At (X (1, "entity"), "h")]),
  REL ("¬", [X (1, "entity")])]))
: Lang.t

With post-processing, restriction material has a placement aligned to the instances of quantification restricted. Such re-organisation cannot occur during the runtime of evaluation since formula material must not fall out of alignment with the state of the sequence assignment.

3.3.4 Closures and (in)definites

Taking `oper`, `l` and `e` as parameters, `closeAll` creates with the primitive `Sct.Close` an `oper` closure with scope over `e`, possibly introducing for the binding names of `l` fresh `Lang.X` sequence values with the accompanying sort information from `l`.

```
val closeAll =
fn oper => fn l => fn e =>
 foldr (
  fn ((x, sort), f) =>
   Sct.Hide (x,
    Sct.Close (oper, (x, sort), rev (map (fn (x, _) => x) l),
     f))) e l
```

Three types of closure will be distinguished, *basic closure*, *discourse level closure* and *question closure*, involving the following binding names with sort information for created bindings:

```
val basic = [
 ("entity", "entity"),
 ("group", "group"),
 ("attrib", "attrib"),
 ("degree", "degree"),
 ("time", "time"),
```

```
 ("event", "event"),
 ("situation", "situation")]

val discourse = [
 ("ENTITY", "entity"),
 ("GROUP", "group"),
 ("ATTRIB", "attrib"),
 ("DEGREE", "degree"),
 ("TIME", "time"),
 ("EVENT", "event"),
 ("SITUATION", "situation")]

val questioned = [
 ("qentity", "entity"),
 ("qgroup", "group"),
 ("qattrib", "attrib"),
 ("qdegree", "degree"),
 ("qtime", "time"),
 ("qevent", "event"),
 ("qsituation", "situation")]
```

closureEnv creates closures with closeAll, having selected the binding names
from l to be closed based on vsort but determined with selectClosures:

```
val selectClosures =
fn vsort => fn l =>
 if member (vsort, discourse) then
  List.filter (fn (x, _) => member (x, l)) (discourse @ basic)
 else if member (vsort, questioned) then
  List.filter (fn (x, _) => member (x, l)) questioned
 else if member (vsort, basic) then
  List.filter (fn (x, _) => member (x, l)) basic
 else
  [vsort]

val closureEnv =
fn oper => fn vsort => fn l => fn e =>
 closeAll oper (selectClosures vsort l) e
```

As an example application of closureEnv, exist brings about a basic existential closure, since ("entity","entity") is a member of basic, restricted to the
members of fh.

```
val exist =
fn fh => fn e =>
 closureEnv "∃" ("entity", "entity") fh e
```

Using `exist` as value for the `env` parameter of `neg` or `md` places a `basic` existential closure directly below the negation operation of `neg` or the modal operation of the `s` parameter of `md`.

```
val neg =
fn fh => fn env => fn e =>
 rel "¬" [env fh e]

val md =
fn fh => fn s => fn env => fn e =>
 rel s [env fh e]
```

To achieve encodings without existential closure, `free` can be given as the value of the `env` parameter.

```
val free =
fn fh => fn e => e
```

With the ability to form closures, an encoding for (in)definites can be defined:

```
val some =
fn lc => fn fh => fn v => fn e1 => fn x => fn e2 =>
 clean x (
   Sct.Use (v, Sct.Lam (v, x,
     manage fh [Sct.Throw (v, NP nil lc e1 x), e2])))
```

Encodings for verbs can also now be assembled with `verb`:

```
val verb =
fn lc => fn event => fn args => fn s =>
 Sct.Use (event,
   predicate lc args [Sct.At (Sct.T (event, 0), event)] s)
```

This builds for a predicate created with `predicate` optional arguments from the local binding names given with the `lc` parameter in addition to required arguments for the names of the `args` parameter together with an extra argument constructed from the name given with the `event` parameter. There is also `Sct.Use` support to ensure the introduction of a fresh `event` binding to be created by the first commanding `event` closure.

It is now possible to analyse (1) as `ex4`.

(1) A boy doesn't like enchiladas.

```
val ex4 =
( fn fh =>
  ( fn lc =>
    ( ( some lc fh "entity"
        ( nn lc "boy"))
      "arg0"
```

```
      ( neg fh exist
        ( ( some lc fh "group"
            ( nn lc "enchiladas"))
          "arg1"
          ( verb lc "event" ["arg0", "arg1"] "does_like")))))
    ["arg1", "arg0", "h"])
["entity", "group", "event"]
```

Evaluation beginning with the empty assignment is possible when ex4 is embedded under a closure for the binding names of the fh parameter: "entity", "group" and "event".

```
> SctToLang.eval (
    fn _ => nil,
    closureEnv "∃" ("ENTITY", "entity")
    ["entity", "group", "event"] ex4);
```
val it =
Quant ("entity", ["event", "group", "entity"], "∃", [X (1, "entity")],
Quant ("group", ["event", "group", "entity"], "∃", [],
Quant ("event", ["event", "group", "entity"], "∃", [],
REL ("", [Throw ("entity", REL ("boy", [At (X (1, "entity"), "h")])),
REL ("¬", [
Quant ("entity", ["event", "group", "entity"], "∃", [],
Quant ("group", ["event", "group", "entity"], "∃", [X (2, "group")],
Quant ("event", ["event", "group", "entity"], "∃", [X (3, "event")],
REL ("", [Throw ("group", REL ("enchiladas", [At (X (2, "group"), "h")])),
REL ("does_like", [At (X (1, "entity"), "arg0"),
At (X (2, "group"), "arg1"),
At (X (3, "event"), "event")])])))))])])))
: Lang.t

Post-processing with Post.transform and Davidsonian.format yields:

```
> Davidsonian.format (Post.transform it);
```
val it =
QUANT ("∃", [X (1, "entity")],
REL ("∧", [REL ("boy", [X (1, "entity")]),
REL ("¬", [
QUANT ("∃", [X (2, "group")],
QUANT ("∃", [X (3, "event")],
REL ("∧", [REL ("enchiladas", [X (2, "group")]),
REL ("does_like", [X (3, "event"), X (1, "entity"),
X (2, "group")])]))])]))])
: Lang.t

The post-processed Lang.t expression pretty printed is as follows:

$\exists x_1 (boy(x_1) \land \neg \exists X_2 e_3 (enchiladas(X_2) \land does\_like(e_3, x_1, X_2)))$

Processing ex4 shows how the scope of an indefinite depends on the placement of closure from where the indefinite receives its binding value. Typically this is the closest commanding instance of existential closure. Negation brings about a basic closure, and because the contribution of *enchiladas* in ex4 appears under the scope of negation the existential binding for *enchiladas* is created by negation. By contrast the contribution of *A boy* is outside the scope of negation and must rely on the initial assignment having an eligible sequence value to shift. Having evaluations begin with a discourse closure (because ("ENTITY", "entity") is a member of discourse but restricted to the names of the fh parameter) ensures the requisite number of sequence values are present.

Definites are distinguishable from indefinites on grounds of receiving bindings that are typically from a discourse closure. Moreover indefinites within the restriction of a definite usually scope with the definite. As an example, consider ex5 as a rendering of (2).

(2) A boy doesn't like the taste of enchiladas.

```
val ex5 =
( fn fh =>
  ( fn lc =>
    ( ( some lc fh "entity"
        ( nn lc "boy"))
      "arg0"
      ( neg fh exist
        ( ( some lc fh "ENTITY"
            ( ( some lc fh "GROUP"
                ( nn lc "enchiladas"))
              "of"
              ( nn lc "taste")))
          "arg1"
          ( verb lc "event" ["arg0", "arg1"] "does_like")))))
  ["of", "arg1", "arg0", "h"])
["entity", "GROUP", "ENTITY", "event"]
```

Evaluation beginning with the empty assignment is possible when ex5 is embedded under closure of "entity", "GROUP", "ENTITY" and "event".

```
> SctToLang.eval (
    fn _ => nil,
    closureEnv "∃" ("ENTITY", "entity")
    ["entity", "GROUP", "ENTITY", "event"] ex5);
```
val it =
Quant ("ENTITY", ["event", "entity", "GROUP", "ENTITY"], "∃", [X (1, "entity")],
Quant ("GROUP", ["event", "entity", "GROUP", "ENTITY"], "∃", [X (2, "group")],
Quant ("entity", ["event", "entity", "GROUP", "ENTITY"], "∃", [X (3, "entity")],
Quant ("event", ["event", "entity", "GROUP", "ENTITY"], "∃", [],

REL ("", [Throw ("entity", REL ("boy", [At (X (3, "entity"), "h")]))),
REL ("¬", [
  Quant ("entity", ["event", "entity"], "∃", [],
   Quant ("event", ["event", "entity"], "∃", [X (4, "event")],
    REL ("", [
     Throw ("ENTITY",
      REL ("", [
       Throw ("GROUP", REL ("enchiladas", [At (X (2, "group"), "h")]))),
       REL ("taste", [At (X (1, "entity"), "h"),
        At (X (2, "group"), "of")])]))),
      REL ("does_like", [At (X (3, "entity"), "arg0"),
       At (X (1, "entity"), "arg1"),
       At (X (4, "event"), "event")])])))])])))))
: Lang.t

Post-processing with `Post.transform` and `Davidsonian.format` yields:

```
> Davidsonian.format (Post.transform it);
```
val it =
QUANT ("∃", [X (1, "entity")],
 QUANT ("∃", [X (2, "group")],
  QUANT ("∃", [X (3, "entity")],
   REL ("∧", [REL ("boy", [X (3, "entity")]),
    REL ("enchiladas", [X (2, "group")]),
    REL ("is_taste_of", [X (1, "entity"), X (2, "group")]),
    REL ("¬", [
     QUANT ("∃", [X (4, "event")],
      REL ("does_like", [X (4, "event"), X (3, "entity"),
       X (1, "entity")])])])])])))
: Lang.t

The post-processed `Lang.t` expression pretty printed is as follows:

$\exists x_1 X_2 x_3 (\text{boy}(x_3) \land \text{enchiladas}(X_2) \land \text{is\_taste\_of}(x_1, X_2) \land$
$\neg \exists e_4 \text{does\_like}(e_4, x_3, x_1))$

Processing ex5 shows discourse level bindings are created for *boy*, *taste* and *enchiladas*. As with ex4, the binding for *boy* obtains because placement is outside the scope of negation. But there are also discourse level bindings for *taste* and *enchiladas*, despite *taste* and *enchiladas* originating from within the scope of negation, as seen from the fact that before `Post.transform` is applied the restriction materials of *taste* and *enchiladas* have placement under negation. The reason for the discourse level bindings of *taste* and *enchiladas* is that these receive bindings created for the "ENTITY" name and "GROUP" name, respectively, both members of `discourse` rather than `basic`, and so not closed by negation. By contrast the "event" binding is created with the `basic` closure of the negation encoding. Following `Post.transform` the level of closure and the level of placement becomes the same for all restriction materials, including *taste* and *enchiladas*.

3.3.5 Proper Names

Proper names lead to individual constants of the target `Lang.t` language, but with a discourse role that may establish accessible antecedents in context. The `Lang.C` individual constant of a proper name is created and given sort information from `sort` and content from `r` with `npr`, and added to the assignment during evaluation given a discourse level of closure with `Sct.CClose ("constant", _)` that gathers the `Lang.C` contribution of `Sct.CUse (_, "constant", _)`. Such gathering leads to the creation of a widely scoped fresh binding that switches to the local binding name of the `x` parameter with `Lang.Lam ("constant", x, _)` when evaluation encounters the proper name itself and subsequently to a contextual binding with coordination or sufficient subordination.

```
val npr =
fn sort => fn r => fn x => fn e =>
 clean x (
  Sct.CUse (Lang.C (r, sort), "constant",
   Sct.Lam ("constant", x, e)))
```

An application of `npr` is demonstrated with the analysis of (3) as `ex6`.

(3) Americans voted for Obama Wednesday.

```
val ex6 =
( fn fh =>
  ( fn lc =>
    ( ( npr "group" "americans")
      "arg0"
      ( ( npr "entity" "obama")
        "for"
        ( ( npr "time" "wednesday")
          "tmp"
          ( verb lc "event" ["arg0", "tmp"] "voted")))))
  ["tmp", "for", "arg0", "arg1", "h"])
["constant", "event"]
```

Here is an evaluation of `ex6`:

```
> SctToLang.eval (
    fn _ => nil,
    Sct.CClose ("constant",
     closureEnv "∃" ("ENTITY", "entity") ["event"] ex6));
val it =
Quant ("event", ["event"], "∃", [X (1, "event")],
 REL ("voted", [At (C ("americans", "group"), "arg0"),
  At (C ("wednesday", "time"), "tmp"), At (C ("obama", "entity"), "for"),
```

At (X (1, "event"), "event")]))
: Lang.t

With post-processing and pretty printing the evaluation result produces:

$$\exists e_1 \, (\text{voted}(e_1, \text{americans}) \wedge \text{tmp}(e_1) = \text{wednesday} \wedge \text{for}(e_1) = \text{obama})$$

The following illustrates how the evaluation proceeds:

```
                        empty assignment
                              |
                Sct.CClose ("constant", _): _
  ["constant" → [C ("americans","group"), C ("obama","entity"), C ("wednesday","time")]  ]
                              |
                 Sct.Hide ("event", _): _
  Sct.Close ("∃","event", ["event"], _): Lang.Quant("event", ["event"], "∃", [X (1, "event")], _)
  ["constant" → [C ("americans","group"), C ("obama","entity"), C ("wednesday","time")]  ]
  ["event" → [X (1, "event")]                                                            ]
                              |
                 Sct.Clean (0, ["arg0"], "c", _): _
                              |
                 Sct.CUse "C ("americans","group")" "constant"
                 Sct.Lam ("constant","arg0", _): _
  ["constant" → [C ("obama","entity"), C ("wednesday","time")]  ]
  ["event" → [X (1, "event")]                                   ]
  ["arg0" → [C ("americans","group")]                           ]
                              |
                 Sct.Clean (0, ["for"], "c", _): _
                              |
                 Sct.CUse "C ("obama","entity")" "constant"
                 Sct.Lam ("constant","for", _): _
  ["constant" → [C ("wednesday","time")]  ]
  ["event" → [X (1, "event")]             ]
  ["arg0" → [C ("americans","group")]     ]
  ["for" → [C ("obama","entity")]         ]
                              |
                 Sct.Clean (0, ["tmp"], "c", _): _
                              |
                 Sct.CUse "C ("wednesday","time")" "constant"
                 Sct.Lam ("constant","tmp", _): _
  ["event" → [X (1, "event")]          ]
  ["arg0" → [C ("americans","group")]  ]
  ["for" → [C ("obama","entity")]      ]
  ["tmp" → [C ("wednesday","time")]    ]
                              |
                 Sct.Use ("event", _): _
                 Sct.If is false: _
                 Sct.If is true: _
                 Sct.If is true: _
                 Sct.Rel ([], [], "voted", _): Lang.REL ("voted", _)
        _____         _____
Sct.At (_, "arg0"): Lang.At (_, "arg0")    /   Sct.At (_, "event"): Lang.At (_, "event")
Sct.T ("arg0", 0): C ("americans","group") /   Sct.T ("event", 0): X (1, "event")

    Sct.At (_, "tmp"): Lang.At (_, "tmp")   Sct.At (_, "for"): Lang.At (_, "for")
    Sct.T ("tmp", 0): C ("wednesday","time") Sct.T ("for", 0): C ("obama","entity")
```

At the start of the evaluation the individual constants of the proper names, made available through Sct.CUse, are entered into the assignment with Sct.CClose as sequence values assigned "constant". A fresh "event" binding is also created, after which the remaining actions with consequences for the assignment involve shifting the assigned sequence values of "constant" to binding names with grammatical roles ("arg0", "for" and "tmp") as the various proper names are reached.

3.3.6 Pronouns

Pronouns typically offer information to limit possible antecedents. For example, *they* should take a group value as antecedent, while *him* should link to an entity value. filter retains potential antecedents of list l that have sort information in list xs.

```
val rec filter =
fn xs => fn l =>
 case l of
   nil => nil
 | Lang.C (s, sort)::r =>
     if member (sort, xs) then Lang.C (s, sort)::filter xs r
     else filter xs r
 | Lang.X (i, sort)::r =>
     if member (sort, xs) then Lang.X (i, sort)::filter xs r
     else filter xs r
 | _::r => filter xs r
```

Pronouns are captured with pro to introduce with Sct.QuantThrow a fresh x binding of sort sort that with post-processing will scope with the commanding v closure. Such a pronoun is resolved by taking as antecedent one of the values that shares sort information with xs and that is gathered with Sct.Pick from the sequences assigned to the names of source at the instance of evaluation (minus x, should this be present in source, which is the case for a reflexive pronoun; see Sect. 4.10)

```
val pro =
fn source => fn fh => fn xs => fn (v, sort) =>
fn s => fn x => fn e =>
 clean x (
   Sct.QuantThrow ((v, sort),
     Sct.Lam (v, x,
       manage fh [
         Sct.Throw (v,
           Sct.Pick (s, Sct.T (x, 0),
             fn l => uniq (filter xs l), diff (source, [x]))), e])))
```

Pronoun use is illustrated with an analysis of (4) as ex7:

(4) Then they supported him.

```
val ex7 =
( fn fh =>
  ( fn lc =>
    ( ( pro ["c"] fh ["group"] ( "group", "group") "they")
      "arg0"
      ( ( pro ["c"] fh ["time"] ( "time", "time") "then")
        "tmp"
        ( ( pro ["c"] fh ["entity"] ( "entity", "entity") "him")
          "arg1"
          ( verb lc "event" ["arg0", "tmp", "arg1"]
            "supported")))))
  ["arg1", "tmp", "arg0", "h"])
["time", "group", "entity", "event"]
```

Antecedents for the three pronouns *they*, *then* and *him* should come from the sequence assigned to "c". Moreover *they* requires as antecedent a variable or constant of Lang.t with "group" sort information; *then*, a "time" antecedent; and *him*, an "entity" antecedent.

An illustration of evaluating the conjunction of ex6 followed by ex7 is as follows:

```
> SctToLang.eval (
    fn _ => nil,
    Sct.CClose ("constant",
      closureEnv "∃" ("ENTITY", "entity")
      ["time", "group", "entity", "event"] (
        Sct.Rel (
          ["constant", "time", "group", "entity", "event"],
          ["c", "c", "c", "c", "c"], "∧", [ex6, ex7])))));
```

val it =
Quant ("entity", ["event", "time", "group", "entity"], "∃", [],
Quant ("group", ["event", "time", "group", "entity"], "∃", [],
 Quant ("time", ["event", "time", "group", "entity"], "∃", [],
  Quant ("event", ["event", "time", "group", "entity"], "∃", [X (2, "event"), X (1,
"event")],
  REL ("∧", [
  REL ("voted", [At (C ("americans", "group"), "arg0"),
  At (C ("wednesday", "time"), "tmp"), At (C ("obama", "entity"), "for"),
  At (X (1, "event"), "event")]),
  QuantThrow ("group", X (3, "group"),
   REL ("", [
   Throw ("group",
   REL ("they:pick", [X (3, "group"), C ("americans", "group")])),

QuantThrow ("time", X (4, "time"),
REL ("", [
Throw ("time",
  REL ("then:pick", [X (4, "time"), C ("wednesday", "time")])),
QuantThrow ("entity", X (5, "entity"),
REL ("", [
Throw ("entity",
  REL ("him:pick", [X (5, "entity"), C ("obama", "entity")])),
REL ("supported", [At (X (3, "group"), "arg0"),
At (X (4, "time"), "tmp"), At (X (5, "entity"), "arg1"),
At (X (2, "event"), "event")])])))])))])))]))))))
: Lang.t

Post-processing the evaluation result repositions the contributions of the pronouns, both the binding introduced with *QuantThrow* as well as the *pick* linking information containing the range of potential antecedents calculated at the instance of evaluation.

```
> Davidsonian.format (Post.transform it);
```
val it =
QUANT ("∃", [X (5, "entity")],
 QUANT ("∃", [X (3, "group")],
  QUANT ("∃", [X (4, "time")],
   QUANT ("∃", [X (2, "event"), X (1, "event")],
    REL ("∧", [
    REL ("then:pick", [X (4, "time"), C ("wednesday", "time")]),
    REL ("they:pick", [X (3, "group"), C ("americans", "group")]),
    REL ("him:pick", [X (5, "entity"), C ("obama", "entity")]),
    REL ("∧", [
    REL ("∧", [REL ("voted", [X (1, "event"), C ("americans", "group")]),
    REL ("=", [REL ("tmp", [X (1, "event")]), C ("wednesday", "time")]),
    REL ("=", [REL ("for", [X (1, "event")]), C ("obama", "entity")])]),
    REL ("∧", [
    REL ("supported", [X (2, "event"), X (3, "group"), X (5, "entity")]),
    REL ("=", [REL ("tmp", [X (2, "event")]), X (4, "time")])])])])])))))
: Lang.t

A pretty print of the result from post-processing is as follows:

$\exists x_5 X_3 t_4 e_1 e_2 (t_4 =$ then{wednesday} $\wedge$ $X_3 =$ they{americans} $\wedge$
$x_5 =$ him{obama} $\wedge$
voted$(e_1,$ americans$)$ $\wedge$ tmp$(e_1) =$ wednesday $\wedge$ for$(e_1) =$ obama $\wedge$
supported(e_2, X_3, x_5) $\wedge$ tmp$(e_2) = t_4)$

A pronoun is resolved when the existentially bound variable introduced by the pronoun is equated to a *pick* variable, seen in curly brackets in the pretty printed version.

3.3.7 *Quantification*

Quantification arises when the trigger for a binding, Sct.Use, is bundled together with a quantificational closure, as with the following definition of every that has parameters to specify the local bindings (lc), the fresh bindings (fh), the binding to be created (v), the sort of the binding to be created (sort), the restriction for the binding (e1), the name under which the binding will bind in the containing clause (x) and the rest of the containing clause (e2).

```
val every =
fn lc => fn fh => fn (v, sort) => fn e1 => fn x => fn e2 =>
 clean x (
   closureEnv "∀" (v, sort) fh (
    Sct.Use (v, Sct.Lam (v, x,
      manage fh [
       Sct.Throw (v, NP nil lc e1 x),
       closureEnv "∃" (v, sort) fh e2]))))
```

Analysis of (5) is now possible with ex8, illustrating an object possessive pronoun under the scope of a quantificational subject with a restriction that contains an indefinite.

(5) Every friend of a farmer likes his donkey.

```
val ex8 =
( fn fh =>
   ( fn lc =>
     ( ( every lc fh ( "entity", "entity")
          ( ( some lc fh "entity"
             ( nn lc "farmer"))
           "of"
           ( nn lc "friend")))
        "arg0"
        ( ( some lc fh "entity"
             ( ( pro ["c"] fh ["entity"] ( "entity", "entity")
                "his")
             "of"
             ( nn lc "donkey")))
          "arg1"
          ( verb lc "event" ["arg0", "arg1"] "likes"))))
  ["of", "arg1", "arg0", "h"])
["entity", "event"]
```

The encoding for *his* positions a pronoun as an "of" binding inside the restriction of an indefinite noun phrase. Internally to the restriction of a noun phrase, all open local bindings of the containing clause shift to be context ("c") bindings, with the exception of the binding created by the noun phrase itself. With local bindings from the containing clause as context bindings, the pronoun within a possessive pronoun construction will have a wider range of binding options than an ordinary non-reflexive pronoun, being able to take as most salient antecedents the bindings from the containing clause that would otherwise have been candidates for a reflexive pronoun, as well as the usual accessible non-local bindings available to a non-reflexive pronoun.

Evaluation of ex8 against the empty assignment and with no additional closures is possible:

```
> SctToLang.eval (fn _ => nil, ex8);
```
val it =
Quant ("entity", ["event", "entity"], "∀", [X (2, "entity"), X (1, "entity")],
Quant ("event", ["event", "entity"], "∀", [],
 REL ("", [
  Throw ("entity",
  REL ("", [Throw ("entity", REL ("farmer", [At (X (1, "entity"), "h")])),
   REL ("friend", [At (X (2, "entity"), "h"), At (X (1, "entity"), "of")])])),
  Quant ("entity", ["event", "entity"], "∃", [X (3, "entity")],
  Quant ("event", ["event", "entity"], "∃", [X (4, "event")],
  REL ("", [
   Throw ("entity",
   QuantThrow ("entity", X (5, "entity"),
   REL ("", [
    Throw ("entity",
    REL ("his:pick", [X (5, "entity"), X (2, "entity"),
    X (1, "entity")])),
    REL ("donkey", [At (X (3, "entity"), "h"),
    At (X (5, "entity"), "of")])]))),
   REL ("likes", [At (X (2, "entity"), "arg0"), At (X (3, "entity"), "arg1"),
   At (X (4, "event"), "event")])])))])))
: Lang.t

Post-processing with Post.transform and Davidsonian.format yields:

```
> Davidsonian.format (Post.transform it);
```
val it =
QUANT ("∀", [X (2, "entity"), X (1, "entity")],
REL ("→", [REL ("farmer", [X (1, "entity")]),
 REL ("is_friend_of", [X (2, "entity"), X (1, "entity")]),
 QUANT ("∃", [X (3, "entity"), X (5, "entity")],
 QUANT ("∃", [X (4, "event")],
  REL ("∧", [
  REL ("his:pick", [X (5, "entity"), X (2, "entity"), X (1, "entity")]),
  REL ("is_donkey_of", [X (3, "entity"), X (5, "entity")]),
  REL ("likes", [X (4, "event"), X (2, "entity"), X (3, "entity")])])))]))
: Lang.t

The post-processed `Lang.t` expression pretty printed is as follows:

$\forall x_1 x_2 (($farmer$(x_1) \land$ is_friend_of$(x_2, x_1)) \rightarrow$
$\quad \exists x_5 x_3 e_4 (x_5 =$ his$\{x_2, x_1\} \land$ is_donkey_of$(x_3, x_5) \land$ likes$(e_4, x_2, x_3)))$

The result from evaluation reveals that the possessive pronoun *his* can be bound either by the same clause subject binding argument *every friend* ... or by *a farmer* contained within the restriction of *every friend* ..., which receives universal quantificational closure from the instance of *every* (that is, a donkey anaphora dependency; Kamp 1981; Barker 1995).

Generalised quantifiers (Barwise and Cooper 1981) can be introduced with `dt` which takes the same range of parameters as `every` but has in addition `oper` to specify the operation of quantification.

```
val dt =
fn lc => fn fh => fn oper => fn (v, sort) =>
fn e1 => fn x => fn e2 =>
 clean x (
  closureEnv oper (v, sort) fh (
   Sct.Use (v, Sct.Lam (v, x,
    manage fh [
     Sct.Throw (v, NP nil lc e1 x),
     closureEnv "∃" (v, sort) fh e2])))))
```

An example with `dt` is given in Sect. 3.3.10.

3.3.8 Verbs with Clause Embedding

Having an embedding poses the danger of inheriting unexpected bindings, for example, from bindings present to support the bound arguments of a predicate that also takes an embedding. To protect embeddings, `subord` is defined to shift to the `"c"` context binding name all sequence values assigned to the names of `lc` minus the names of `keep`:

```
val subord =
fn lc => fn keep => fn e =>
 Sct.Clean (0, diff (lc, keep), "c", e)
```

Constructing a clause embedding as an argument with grammatical role information can be accomplished with `that`, which keeps none of the open bindings for the names of `lc`.

```
val that =
fn lc => fn e =>
 Sct.At (subord lc nil e, "that")
```

embVerb captures verbs that take an embedding, with the embedding integrated as an extra argument for a call of predicate.

```
val embVerb =
fn lc => fn event => fn args => fn s => fn e =>
 Sct.Use (event,
  predicate lc args [
   Sct.At (Sct.T (event, 0), event),
   Sct.Lam (event, "cevent", e)] s)
```

In addition to required arguments established with the args and event parameters, predicate ensures there are bound arguments for any other open local bindings. The definition also integrates before the embedding clearing to the privileged "cevent" context binding name of the binding name given with the event parameter, which receives Sct.Use support.

As an example of embVerb followed by that, consider:

(6) On Monday John thought that Mary left.

An encoding for (6) is given as ex9.

```
val ex9 =
( fn fh =>
  ( fn lc =>
    ( ( npr "entity" "john")
      "arg0"
      ( ( npr "time" "monday")
        "on"
        ( embVerb lc "event" ["arg0"] "thought"
          ( that lc
            ( ( npr "entity" "mary")
              "arg0"
              ( verb lc "event" ["arg0"] "left")))))))
  ["arg0", "that", "on", "arg1", "h"])
["constant", "event"]
```

Evaluation beginning with the empty assignment is possible when ex9 is under an instance of Sct.CClose that collects values for the "constant" name as well as an "event" closure:

```
> SctToLang.eval (
    fn _ => nil,
    Sct.CClose ("constant",
     closureEnv "∃" ("ENTITY", "entity") ["event"] ex9));
```
val it =
Quant ("event", ["event"], "∃", [X (2, "event"), X (1, "event")],
REL ("thought", [At (C ("john", "entity"), "arg0"),
At (C ("monday", "time"), "on"), At (X (2, "event"), "event"),

At (
REL ("left", [At (C ("mary", "entity"), "arg0"),
At (X (1, "event"), "event")]), "that")]))
: Lang.t

With post-processing and pretty printing the evaluation result produces:

$\exists e_1 e_2 \, (\text{thought}(e_2, \text{ john}, \text{ left}(e_1, \text{ mary})) \wedge \text{on}(e_2) = \text{monday})$

What happens can be illustrated as follows, picking up evaluation after the initial existential closure that leaves two sequence elements assigned to "event" and after the opening of "arg0" and "on" bindings from the matrix arguments:

```
                    ["event" → [X (2, "event"), X (1, "event")]]
                    ["arg0"  → [C ("john","entity")]
                    ["on"    → [C ("monday","time")]
                    ["constant" → [C ("mary","entity")]]

                              |
                    Sct.Use ("event", _): _
                      Sct.If is true: _
                      Sct.If is false: _
                      Sct.If is true: _
                      Sct.If is true: _
            Sct.Rel ([], [], "thought", _): Lang.REL ("thought", _)

Sct.At (_, "arg0"): Lang.At (_, "arg0")                          Sct.Lam ("event","cevent", _): _
Sct.T ("arg0", 0): C ("john","entity")                          ["event" → [X (1, "event")]
                                                                ["arg0"  → [C ("john","entity")]]
        Sct.At (_, "on"): Lang.At (_, "on")                     ["cevent" → [X (2, "event")]
        Sct.T ("on", 0): C ("monday","time")                    ["on"    → [C ("monday","time")]
                                                                ["constant" → [C ("mary","entity")]]
              Sct.At (_, "event"): Lang.At (_, "event")                      |
              Sct.T ("event", 0): X (2, "event")        Sct.At (_, "that"): Lang.At (_, "that")
                                              Sct.Clean (0, ["arg0","that","on","arg1","h"], "c", _): _
                                              ["event" → [X (1, "event")]
                                              ["cevent" → [X (2, "event")]
                                              ["c" → [C ("monday","time"), C ("john","entity")]
                                              ["constant" → [C ("mary","entity")]]
                                                              |
                                              Sct.Clean (0, ["arg0"], "c", _): _
                                                              |
                                              Sct.CUse "C ("mary","entity")" "constant"
                                                Sct.Lam ("constant","arg0", _): _
                                              ["event" → [X (1, "event")]
                                              ["arg0"  → [C ("mary","entity")]
                                              ["cevent" → [X (2, "event")]
                                              ["c" → [C ("monday","time"), C ("john","entity")]]
                                                              |
                                                Sct.Use ("event", _): _
                                                  Sct.If is true: _
                                                  Sct.If is true: _
                                                  Sct.If is true: _
                                                  Sct.If is true: _
                                              Sct.Rel ([], [], "left", _): Lang.REL ("left", _)

                            Sct.At (_, "arg0"): Lang.At (_, "arg0")Sct.At (_, "event"): Lang.At (_, "event")
                            Sct.T ("arg0", 0): C ("mary","entity")  Sct.T ("event", 0): X (1, "event")
```

The "on" binding has a created argument of the embedding predicate to bind. Together with the "arg0" binding, the "on" binding shifts to be part of the sequence assigned "c" for the evaluation of the embedding. Also the first sequence value of the "event" binding of the initial assignment state shifts to a "cevent" binding, while the second sequence value binds into the embedding.

3.3.9 Control Embedding

What marks out control (see e.g., Landau 2013) as a construction that differs from ordinary embedding is that an obligatory dependency is established between an argument of the embedding predicate and the embedded clause, as the examples of (7) demonstrate.

(7) a. John needed to go.
    b. John needed Mary to go.

An obligatory dependency is assured when (shifted) bindings are established with the same assigned sequence element. Control dependencies are captured with preservation of a local binding of the embedding predicate into the embedding, including the possibility of a shift to a different local binding name, e.g., with (7b) what is the "arg1" binding of the embedding predicate should be the "arg0" binding for the embedding. Such preservation is accomplished with control:

```
val control =
fn lc => fn e =>
 Sct.Clean (0, ["arg1", "lgs", "arg2"], "arg0",
   subord lc ["arg0", "arg1", "arg2"] (
    Sct.If (fn g: Lang.t Assign.t => null (g "arg0"),
     e,
     Sct.Clean (1, ["arg0"], "c", e))))
```

All sequence values assigned to "arg1", then "lgs" (binding for a logical subject, possibly present with passives; see Sect. 4.4) and then "arg2" shift to the "arg0" binding. There is then removal (to "c") with subord of any sequence values assigned to names of the lc parameter except "arg0", "arg1" and "arg2". Finally if "arg0" is non-empty there is removal to "c" of all assigned values except the frontmost value.

Control integrated into a clause embedding as an argument with grammatical role information is accomplished with toComp:

```
val toComp =
fn lc => fn e =>
 Sct.At (control lc e, "toComp")
```

To illustrate toComp occurring with embVerb, consider ex10 as an encoding for (7a) and ex11 for (7b).

```
val ex10 =
( fn fh =>
  ( fn lc =>
    ( ( npr "entity" "john")
      "arg0"
      ( embVerb lc "event" ["arg0"] "needed"
        ( toComp lc
```

```
              ( verb lc "event" nil "go")))))
   ["toComp", "arg0", "arg1", "h"])
["constant", "event"]

val ex11 =
( fn fh =>
  ( fn lc =>
    ( ( npr "entity" "john")
      "arg0"
      ( ( npr "entity" "mary")
        "arg1"
        ( embVerb lc "event" ["arg0", "arg1"] "needed"
          ( toComp lc
            ( verb lc "event" nil "go"))))))
   ["toComp", "arg1", "arg0", "h"])
["constant", "event"]
```

Having ex10 under Sct.CClose collecting values for the "constant" name and an "event" closure permits evaluation:

```
> SctToLang.eval (
    fn _ => nil,
    Sct.CClose ("constant",
      closureEnv "∃" ("ENTITY", "entity") ["event"] ex10));
```
val it =
Quant ("event", ["event"], "∃", [X (2, "event"), X (1, "event")],
REL ("needed", [At (C ("john", "entity"), "arg0"), At (X (2, "event"), "event"),
At (
REL ("go", [At (C ("john", "entity"), "arg0"), At (X (1, "event"), "event")]),
"toComp")]))
: Lang.t

With post-processing and pretty printing the evaluation result produces:

$\exists e_1 e_2$ needed $(e_2,$ john, go $(e_1,$ john$))$

This success can be illustrated as follows, picking up evaluation after the initial existential closure that leaves two sequence elements assigned to "event" and after the opening of the "arg0" binding from the matrix argument:

```
                    ["event" → [X (2, "event"), X (1, "event")]
                     "argo" → [C ("john","entity")]                ]
                                        |
                          Sct.Use ("event", _): _
                              Sct.If is true: _
                              Sct.If is true: _
                              Sct.If is true: _
                    Sct.Rel ([], [], "needed", _): Lang.REL ("needed", _)
                   _____|_____
                  /                        |                \
Sct.At (_, "argo"): Lang.At (_, "argo")          Sct.Lam ("event","cevent", _): _
Sct.T ("argo", 0): C ("john","entity")           ["event" → [X (1, "event")]
                                                  "argo" → [C ("john","entity")]
         Sct.At (_, "event"): Lang.At (_, "event")  "cevent" → [X (2, "event")]  ]
             Sct.T ("event", 0): X (2, "event")              |
                          Sct.At (_, "toComp"): Lang.At (_, "toComp")
                     Sct.Clean (0, ["arg1","lgs","arg2"], "argo", _): _
                                        |
                          Sct.Clean (0, ["toComp","h"], "c", _): _
                                        |
                              Sct.If is false: _
                          Sct.Clean (1, ["argo"], "c", _): _
                                        |
                              Sct.Use ("event", _): _
                                  Sct.If is true: _
                                  Sct.If is false: _
                                  Sct.If is true: _
                                  Sct.If is true: _
                          Sct.Rel ([], [], "go", _): Lang.REL ("go", _)
                   _____|_____
                  /                                          \
Sct.At (_, "argo"): Lang.At (_, "argo")  Sct.At (_, "event"): Lang.At (_, "event")
Sct.T ("argo", 0): C ("john","entity")     Sct.T ("event", 0): X (1, "event")
```

Because clearing happens with `toComp`, which allows for the most recent addition to the sequence assigned `"argo"` to remain as the sole sequence element assigned `"argo"`, there is actually no alteration to the assignment on entry to the embedding.

Having `ex11` under `Sct.CClose` collecting values for the `"constant"` name and an `"event"` closure permits evaluation:

```
> SctToLang.eval (
    fn _ => nil,
    Sct.CClose ("constant",
      closureEnv "∃" ("ENTITY", "entity") ["event"] ex11));
val it =
Quant ("event", ["event"], "∃", [X (2, "event"), X (1, "event")],
REL ("needed", [At (C ("john", "entity"), "argo"),
At (C ("mary", "entity"), "arg1"), At (X (2, "event"), "event"),
At (
  REL ("go", [At (C ("mary", "entity"), "argo"), At (X (1, "event"), "event")]),
  "toComp")]))
: Lang.t
```

With post-processing and pretty printing the evaluation result produces:

$$\exists e_1 e_2 \text{needed}(e_2, \text{john}, \text{mary}, \text{go}(e_1, \text{mary}))$$

This success can be illustrated as follows, picking up evaluation after the initial existential closure that leaves two sequence elements assigned to "event" and after the opening of "arg0" and "arg1" bindings from the matrix arguments:

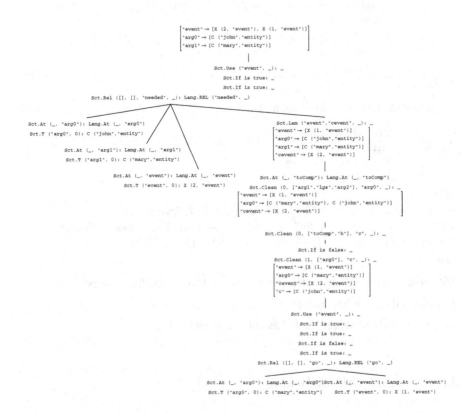

With clearing brought about by toComp, there is first a shift of the "arg1" binding to become the most recent addition of the sequence assigned "arg0" which is subsequently preserved into the embedding, while what had begun as the sole element assigned "arg0" shifts to the "c" binding that stores accessible bindings of the discourse context.

A control dependency is broken if there is an intervening subject noun phrase. Thus, expletive *it* occurs in (8) and *John* does not bind into the infinitive embedding, in contrast to (7a).

(8) John needed it to rain.

Suppose expletive *it* contributes clean only, to bring about the clearing associated with the creation of a new argument binding without introducing a new binding. A rendering of (8) can be given as ex12:

```
val ex12 =
( fn fh =>
  ( fn lc =>
    ( ( npr "entity" "john")
      "arg0"
      ( embVerb lc "event" ["arg0"] "needed"
        ( toComp lc
          ( ( clean "arg0")
            ( verb lc "event" nil "rain"))))))
  ["toComp", "arg0", "arg1", "h"])
["constant", "event"]
```

The following illustrates evaluation of ex12:

```
> SctToLang.eval (
    fn _ => nil,
    Sct.CClose ("constant",
      closureEnv "∃" ("ENTITY", "entity") ["event"] ex12));
```
val it =
Quant ("event", ["event"], "∃", [X (2, "event"), X (1, "event")],
REL ("needed", [At (C ("john", "entity"), "arg0"), At (X (2, "event"), "event"),
At (REL ("rain", [At (X (1, "event"), "event")]), "toComp")]))
: Lang.t

With post-processing and pretty printing the evaluation result produces:

$\exists e_1 e_2 \text{needed} (e_2, \text{john}, \text{rain}(e_1))$

Notably the embedded predicate has only an event binding.

3.3.10 Nouns with Embedding

Having nouns with embedding is achieved with embNn. Before the embedding occurs the sequence value assigned "h" shifts to " ". Once assigned to " " a value is essentially removed from further consideration.

```
val embNn =
fn lc => fn s => fn e =>
 predicate lc ["h"] [Sct.Lam ("h", "", e)] s
```

As an example of embNn applied, consider (9):

(9)   arranged in such a way that information emerges

An encoding for (9) is offered by ex13, with the embedded clause integrated with embNn and that (see Sect. 3.3.8).

```
val ex13 =
( fn fh =>
  ( fn lc =>
    ( ( dt lc fh "SUCH" ( "such", "entity")
        ( embNn lc "way"
          ( that lc
            ( ( some lc fh "entity"
                ( nn lc "information"))
              "arg0"
              ( verb lc "event" ["arg0"] "emerges")))))
      "in"
      ( verb lc "event" nil "arranged")))
  ["arg0", "that", "in", "arg1", "h"])
["entity", "event", "such"]
```

The following demonstrates evaluation of ex13:

```
> SctToLang.eval (
    fn _ => nil,
    closureEnv
      "∃" ("ENTITY", "entity") ["entity", "event", "such"] ex13);
```
val it =
Quant ("entity", ["event", "entity"], "∃", [X (1, "entity")],
  Quant ("event", ["event", "entity"], "∃", [X (3, "event"), X (2, "event")],
  Quant ("such", ["such"], "SUCH", [X (4, "entity")],
  REL ("", [
  Throw ("such",
  REL ("way", [At (X (4, "entity"), "h"),
  At (
  REL ("", [
  Throw ("entity", REL ("information", [At (X (1, "entity"), "h")])),
  REL ("emerges", [At (X (1, "entity"), "arg0"),
  At (X (2, "event"), "event")])]), "that")])),
  Quant ("such", ["such"], "∃", [],
  REL ("arranged", [At (X (4, "entity"), "in"),
  At (X (3, "event"), "event")])])])))))
: Lang.t

Post-processing the evaluation result repositions restriction materials with *informa-tion* receiving placement outside the embedding.

```
> Davidsonian.format (Post.transform it);
```
val it =
QUANT ("∃", [X (1, "entity")],
  QUANT ("∃", [X (3, "event"), X (2, "event")],
  REL ("∧", [REL ("information", [X (1, "entity")]),
  QUANT ("SUCH", [X (4, "entity")],

REL ("", [
REL ("is_way_that", [X (4, "entity"),
REL ("emerges", [X (2, "event"), X (1, "entity")])]),
REL ("∧", [REL ("arranged", [X (3, "event")]),
REL ("=", [REL ("in", [X (3, "event")]), X (4, "entity")])])])))])))
: Lang.t

A pretty print of the result from post-processing is as follows:

$\exists x_1 e_2 e_3$ (information (x_1) ∧

SUCHx_4 (is_way_that $(x_4,$ emerges $(e_2,$ $x_1))$, arranged (e_3) ∧ in (e_3) $=$ $x_4)$)

3.4 Summary

This chapter has developed the idea that evaluation itself can shoulder much of the
burden of automatically determining when, where and how binding dependencies are
established, not only by selecting what are the appropriate predicate-argument structures, as in Chap. 2, but also by governing the release and subsequent accessibility of
bindings. The results of this chapter crucially exploit the very moment of evaluation,
which is revealed to be the one instance in the processing a linguistic expression
when a maximum of information is available, regarding what has happened with the
accessible history of bindings, but also regarding what has yet to happen with the
countable morphosyntax of the expression content that remains to be evaluated.

References

Barker C (1995) Possessive descriptions. CSLI Publications, Stanford

Barwise J, Cooper R (1981) Generalized quantifiers and natural languages. Linguist Philos 4:159–
219

Kamp H (1981) A theory of truth and semantic representation. In: Groenendijk J, Janssen T, Stokhof
M (eds) Formal methods in the study of language. Mathematical Centre, Amsterdam, pp 277–322

Landau I (2013) Control in generative grammar: a research companion. Cambridge University
Press, Cambridge

Chapter 4
Treebank Annotation

This chapter presents treebank annotation that with modest conversion serves as a syntactic base for feeding the SCT evaluation mechanism of the previous chapter. The chapter has three goals:

- to detail the annotation scheme,
- to sketch how annotation is converted to an SCT expression, and
- to observe meaning representations that follow from the annotations/SCT expressions.

Annotation will follow the *Annotation manual for the Penn Historical Corpora and the Parsed Corpus of Early English Correspondence (PCEEC)* (Santorini 2010), hereafter referred to as the annotation system. Representing syntactic structure with labelled parentheses, the annotation system is a modified Penn Treebank scheme (Bies et al. 1995), closely related to the *Penn-Helsinki Parsed Corpus of Middle English II (PPCME2)* scheme (Taylor 1999). Differences from the Penn Treebank scheme include cosmetic changes to give nodes of parsed trees labels that are familiar to generative linguists. There are also major changes: the VP level of structure is absent except with conjunction, the internal syntax of phrasal categories is fundamentally similar, and function is marked on all clausal nodes and all NPs that are clause level constituents, but not on PPs.

The chapter is structured as follows. Section 4.1 outlines the general principles followed in parsing with the annotation system and presents common structures. The aim is to retain compatibility with the existing annotation system and so with available corpora (e.g., Kroch et al. 2010). Section 4.2 discusses emergence as well as manipulation of a default scope hierarchy from the flat clause level annotation. Section 4.3 sketches how parsed annotations can be converted into SCT expressions. Subsequent sections (Sects. 4.7–4.21) illustrate the broad coverage that is achieved with examples of passives, adverbial clauses, participial clauses, adjectives, adverbs, floating quantifiers, pronominal binding, covaluation arising because of embedding, wh-questions, relative clauses, free relative clauses, comparative clauses, tough movement complements, clause-adjoined relative clauses, phrasal conjunction, speech parentheticals, and nouns of address. Section 4.22 provides a summary.

© Springer International Publishing Switzerland 2015
A. Butler, *Linguistic Expressions and Semantic Processing*,
DOI 10.1007/978-3-319-18830-0_4

4.1 General Parsing Principles

The annotation system represents syntactic structure with labelled parentheses. All open parentheses have an associated label, representing nodes in a tree. Labels are either word level part-of-speech tags (N, P, ADJ, etc.), or phrase level categories (NP, PP, ADJP, etc.). There is typically no specified VP level, so clause structure is generally flat with multiply branching nodes, with IP-MAT (a matrix IP) immediately dominating all verbs (to be understood in a broad sense, including modals and auxiliaries) and sentence level constituents. A typical parse in tree form looks like:

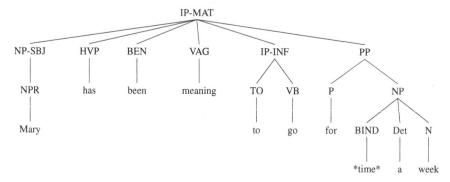

In bracketed notation this is:

```
(IP-MAT (NP-SBJ (NPR Mary))
        (HVP has)
        (BEN been)
        (VAG meaning)
        (IP-INF (TO to)
                (VB go))
        (PP (P for)
            (NP (BIND *time*)
                (D a)
                (N week))))
```

Being additional to the annotation system, tag BIND influences the sort of a binding when placed within the noun phrase that acts to create the binding, as for example with (BIND *time*).

Every word has a word level part-of-speech label. Phrasal labels are not included in every case in which a fully labelled tree would require them. Intermediate levels of structure in the sense of X' theory (N', ADJ', etc.) are never represented explicitly. Thus in the annotation system, the phrasal node (NP, PP, ADJP, etc.) immediately dominates the phrase head (N, P, ADJ, etc.) and both modifiers and complements are sisters of the head:

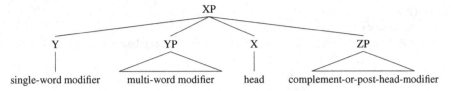

single-word modifier   multi-word modifier   head   complement-or-post-head-modifier

In general the head (N, P, ADJ, etc.) is overt and matches the category of the phrase
level (NP, PP, ADJP, etc.).

```
(PP (P in)
    (NP (D the)
        (N spring)))

(ADJP (ADVP (ADVR so)
            (ADV absurdly))
      (ADJ unreasonable))
```

The lack of a word level constituent to match the phrase in category indicates either
(i) the head has been elided (which is not indicated); or (ii) the head has a more
specific label than its general category label.

```
(NP (D these))   ← elided case

(NP (PRO 'em))   ← more specific label case
```

With two exceptions, heads always project a phrasal node. First certain heads,
such as D (determiner), NEG (negation), RP (particle), Q (floated quantifier) and all
verbs (including modals and auxiliaries), never project a phrase. The second case
involves single-word pre-head modifiers; these do not project a phrasal node when
that node is predictable from the word level annotation (e.g., ADJP is predictable
from ADJ). All multi-worded pre-head modifiers project phrasal nodes. Because of
the lack of intermediate levels of structure, all modifiers appear as sisters of the head.

```
(NP (D a)
    (ADJ big)   ← single-word case
    (N cat))

(NP (D a)
    (ADJP (ADV very)   ← multi-word case
          (ADJ big))
    (N cat))
```

Complements and post-head modifiers always project a phrasal node, whether
they consist of a single word or not. Like pre-head modifiers, they are sisters to the
head.

```
(NP (N Fish)
    (ADJP (ADJR enough)))   ← post-head modifier
```

```
(NP (D a)
    (N doubt)
    (CP-THT (C that)                          ← complement
            (IP-SUB (NP-SBJ (PRO it))
                    (BED was)
                    (NEG not))))
```

In addition to verbal material (auxiliaries, modals, verbs, participles), a small number of other word level constituents can be immediately dominated by IP. These are: sentential conjunctions (CONJ and some cases of ALSO, ELSE), single-word interjections (INTJ), sentential negation (NEG), and adverbial particles (RP).

```
(IP-MAT (CONJ And)                    ← sentential conjunction
        (NP-SBJ (NPR Mary))
        (VBD looked)
        (RP up)                       ← particle
        (NP-OB1 (NPR$ Jane's)
                (N number)))
```

The annotation system labels for both form and function. In general, the basic label indicates the form of the constituent (NP, PP, ADJP, etc.), while additional labels (separated by a hyphen) indicate function (NP-SBJ = subject, ADVP-TMP = temporal adverb, ADJP-SPR = secondary predicate adjective phrase, CP-REL = relative clause, IP-INF = infinitive, etc.). Not all constituents are marked for function; in most cases there is at most one additional label, but there may be more (IP-INF-PRP = purpose infinitive, IP-IMP-SPE = direct speech imperative, etc.).

All noun phrases immediately dominated by IP are marked for function (NP-SBJ = subject, NP-OB1 = direct object, NP-OB2 = indirect object, NP-MSR = measure NP, NP-TMP = temporal NP, etc.). NPs without functional information are either complements of a non-verbal head (e.g., a preposition), or part of a conjunction structure.

```
(IP-MAT (NP-TMP (N Yesterday))
        (NP-SBJ (NPR Mary))
        (VBD told)
        (NP-OB2 (NPR Jane))
        (CP-THT (C that)
                (IP-SUB (NP-SBJ (PRO she))
                        (VBD studied)
                        (NP-MSR (QP (ADVR too)
                                    (Q much)))
                        (PP (P during)
                            (NP (D the)
                                (N+N weekend))))))

(IP-MAT (NP-SBJ (NP (ADJ Fresh)
                    (N hope))
```

```
                    (CONJP (CONJ and)
                           (NP (VAN renewed)
                               (N vigour))))
          (VBD prevailed)
          (. ,))
```

Argument and adjunct PPs are not distinguished, nor are any PPs marked for function.

```
(IP-MAT (NP-SBJ (NPR Mary))
        (VBD put)
        (NP-OB1 (D the)
                (N book))
        (PP (P on)                    ← argument PP
            (NP (D the)
                (N table)))
        (PP (P for)                   ← adjunct PP
            (NP (NPR Jane))))
```

Only locative, temporal and directional adverb phrases are marked for function; others are unmarked.

```
(IP-MAT (NP-SBJ (NPR Mary))
        (ADVP (ADV happily))
        (VBD put)
        (NP-OB1 (D the)
                (N book))
        (ADVP-LOC (ADV there))
        (ADVP-TMP (ADV+WARD afterward)))
```

All clauses have extended labels. Matrix clauses are labelled IP-MAT; they may be further characterised as direct speech (IP-MAT-SPE) or parentheticals (IP-MAT-PRN, see Sect. 4.19). Clauses with a complementiser position are labelled IP-SUB. Other clauses without a complementiser position are labelled IP and further labelled for function:

complement infinitive IP-INF
purpose infinitive IP-INF-PRP
adjunct infinitive IP-INF-ADT
small clause IP-SMC
participial clause IP-PPL
absolute IP-ABS

All CP clauses project a CP node with extended label to indicate function. The following (see Sects. 4.12–4.17 for examples) also include a wh-constituent (WNP, WADJP, WADVP, WPP) that may be overt or empty and an associated trace (*T*):

wh-questions (direct or indirect) CP-QUE
relative clauses CP-REL
free relative clauses CP-FRL

clause-adjoined relative CP-CAR
comparative clauses CP-CMP
some adverbial clauses CP-ADV
tough-movement complements CP-TMC
it-cleft CP-CLF

When empty, the wh-constituent content is represented by 0 (i.e., zero). The trace is always the first element in the IP complement, irrespective of its function. All these CPs except direct questions and infinitival relatives also include a complementiser position (C), which may be overt or empty. An empty complementiser is represented by 0.

In the remaining types of CP clauses the complementiser position is always indicated (whether overt or empty) but there is no wh-element at the CP level.

yes/no questions CP-QUE
that complements CP-THT
adverbial clauses CP-ADV
degree clauses CP-DEG

4.2 Clause Level Scope Annotation

Because structure is generally flat at the clause level where scope relationships are in principle most free, there is no structural enforcement of scope relations. Nevertheless when there are multiple modifiers some exact ordering should be determined. Linear precedence is one basis for a default ordering, with prior modifiers taking wider scope.

In addition to linear precedence, several other properties impinge on a default scope arrangement. Most notably, whatever acts as the predicate of the clause, irrespective of linear precedence, must be lowest in the scope hierarchy, with the exception of any complement, which must be lower still. Additionally, certain modifiers will, owing to functional marking, demand a widest scope placement, e.g., topic (-TPC) or vocative (-VOC, see Sect. 4.21) marked arguments. Finally, it is helpful to assume arguments tagged -SBJ (subject) have a scope placement above other modifiers by default, and that participial clauses (IP-PPL, see Sect. 4.6) and phrases acting as secondary predicates (e.g., ADJP-SPR, see Sect. 4.7) remain below subjects. Thereby subjects always have the prospect of binding through to participial clauses and secondary predicates irrespective of linear precedence.

With the above considerations for determining a default scope placement, only deviations need to be explicitly marked, to be accomplished with two dash tags that are additional to the annotation system, -HIGH and -LOW, with the resulting hierarchy:

                                                                    WIDEST SCOPE
modifier tagged -TPC, -VOC or -HIGH (except with IP-PPL or -SPR)
    argument tagged SBJ
        IP-PPL or -SPR with -HIGH
            placement of MD
                placement of negation
                    default placement of modifier untagged for scope
                        modifier tagged -LOW
                            predicate
NARROWEST SCOPE   complement

When multiple modifiers share the same scope dash tag, e.g., two modifiers are marked -LOW, then linear precedence determines the relative scoping.

4.3 Conversion

The uniformity of phrase structure imposed by the annotation system is exploited when converting tree structures into SCT expressions. This can be demonstrated with a short awk program (Aho et al. 1988) to capture the essence of a program used for conversion. The main routine phrase accepts the content of a phrase given as a string with constituents separated by a given divider (typically the phrase label enclosed by @) and returns an expression assembled from the constituents. For example:

```
phrase("@XP@", "(m m1)@XP@(m m2)@XP@(h h)@XP@(c c)")
phrase("@XP@", "(m m)@XP@(h h)@XP@(c c)")
phrase("@XP@", "(c c)@XP@(m m)@XP@(h h)")
phrase("@XP@", "(h h)@XP@(c c)")
phrase("@XP@", "(m m)@XP@(c c)")
phrase("@XP@", "(m m)@XP@(h h)")
phrase("@XP@", "(c c)")
phrase("@XP@", "(h h)")
phrase("@XP@", "(m m)")
```

returns

```
(XP (MOD m1) ((MOD m2) ((HEAD h) (COMP c))))
(XP (MOD m) ((HEAD h) (COMP c)))
(XP (MOD m) ((HEAD h) (COMP c)))
(XP (HEAD h) (COMP c))
(XP (MOD m) (COMP c))
(XP (MOD m) ((HEAD h)))
(XP COMP c)
(XP (HEAD h))
(XP (MOD m) (DEFAULT_HEAD))
```

COMP, HEAD and MOD of the output are placeholders for adding material relevant to the type of phrase and processed content. Routine phrase works by passing the embedded constituents to and collecting results from the routines of embedding, head and `modifier`. A warning is given if there are unincorporated constituents after the `modifier` call.

```
# main routine
function phrase(divider,e)
{
  e = embedding(divider, e)
  e = head(divider,
   part(2, "__EMBEDDING__", e), part(1, "__EMBEDDING__", e))
  e = modifier(divider,
   part(2, "__HEAD__", e), part(1, "__HEAD__", e))
  # warn of remaining elements
  if (part(2, "__COMPLETED__", e))
  {
    print "WARNING:" part(2, "__COMPLETED__", e)
  }
  return (sprintf ("(%s %s)",
   gensub(/@/, "", "g", divider), part(1, "__COMPLETED__", e)))
}

# auxiliary routines
function part(n,divider,e, parts)
{
  split (e, parts, divider)
  return (parts[n])
}
function node(s)
{
  return (gensub(/^\(/, "", 1, gensub(/ .*$/, "", 1, s)))
}
function remove(c,s)
{
  if (index(s, "(" c ")"))
  {
    s = gensub(/\)$/, "", 1, substr(s, length(c) + 3))
  }
  return (s)
}
```

The purpose of `embedding` is to find if there is a constituent with a complement role by matching an element with a certain node label (here c; but generally dependent on the phrase type). Output is given as two strings separated by __EMBEDDING__, where the first is the (possibly empty) embedding and the second (also possibly empty) contains those constituents of the phrase that await processing.

```
# discover complement
function embedding(divider,e, goal,e_parts,n_parts,i,rest)
```

```
{
  n_parts = split (e, e_parts, divider)
  for (i = 1; i <= n_parts; i++)
  {
    if (e_parts[i] ~ /^\(c /)
    {
      goal = sprintf ("COMP %s",
        remove(node(e_parts[i]), e_parts[i]))
    }
    else
    {
      rest = sprintf("%s%s%s",
        rest, rest ? divider : "", e_parts[i])
    }
  }
  return (goal "__EMBEDDING__" rest)
}
```

The head routine finds the head of the phrase by matching a certain node label (here h; dependent on the phrase type). When a value for goal exists (which will be an embedding found with the prior call of embedding), then this is included with the found head as the new goal value. After looking for the head, if goal still lacks a value then a default value specific to the phrase type is given as the value of goal. The goal value is then returned separated by __HEAD__ from the phrase elements that remain to be processed.

```
# establish head
function head(divider,e,goal, e_parts,n_parts,i,rest)
{
  n_parts = split (e, e_parts, divider)
  for (i = 1; i <= n_parts; i++)
  {
    if (e_parts[i] ~ /^\(h /)
    {
      if (goal)
      {
        goal = sprintf("(HEAD %s) (%s)",
          remove(node(e_parts[i]), e_parts[i]), goal)
      }
      else
      {
        goal = sprintf("(HEAD %s)",
          remove(node(e_parts[i]), e_parts[i]))
      }
    }
    else
```

```
    {
      rest = sprintf("%s%s%s",
        rest, rest ? divider : "", e_parts[i])
    }
  }
  # if goal missing create default
  if (!goal)
  {
    goal = "DEFAULT_HEAD"
  }
  return (goal "__HEAD__" rest)
}
```

The modifier routine adds modifiers as elements that take scope over the head.

```
# add modifiers
function modifier(divider,e,goal, e_parts,n_parts,i,rest)
{
  n_parts = split (e, e_parts, divider)
  for (i = n_parts; i >= 1; i--)
  {
    if (e_parts[i] ~ /^\(m /)
    {
      goal = sprintf("(MOD %s) (%s)",
        remove(node(e_parts[i]), e_parts[i]), goal)
    }
    else
    {
      rest = sprintf("%s%s%s",
        rest, rest ? divider : "", e_parts[i])
    }
  }
  return (goal "__COMPLETED__" rest)
}
```

As a demonstration, consider the first example of Sect. 4.1, repeated in bracketed notation:

```
(IP-MAT (NP-SBJ (NPR Mary))
        (HVP has)
        (BEN been)
        (VAG meaning)
        (IP-INF (TO to)
                (VB go))
        (PP (P for)
            (NP (BIND *time*)
                (D a)
                (N week))))
```

An SCT expression is built by sending each phrase level to versions of `phrase` that are specific to the phrase type, assembling SCT expression materials as described above, as well as information about the local binding names, with the following intermediate results:

```
NP-SBJ-in: (NPR mary)

NP-SBJ-out: (NP-SBJ npr "entity" "mary"__LOCAL__)

IP-INF-in: (TO to)@IP-INF@(VB go)

IP-INF-out: (IP-INF-to verb lc "event" nil "go"__LOCAL__)

NP-in: (D a)@NP@(N week)

NP-out: (NP some lc fh "time" (nn lc "week")__LOCAL__)

PP-in: (P for)@PP@(NP some lc fh "time" (nn lc "week")__LOCAL__)

PP-out: (PP-NP (some lc fh "time" (nn lc "week")) "for"__LOCAL__
        "for")
```

With the IP level, elements are organised to follow the hierarchy of Sect. 4.2:

```
IP-MAT-in: (NP-SBJ npr "entity" "mary"__LOCAL__)@IP-MAT@(HVP has)
           @IP-MAT@(BEN been)@IP-MAT@(VAG meaning)@IP-MAT@
           (IP-INF-to verb lc "event" nil "go"__LOCAL__)@IP-MAT@
           (PP-NP (some lc fh "time" (nn lc "week")) "for"
           __LOCAL__"for")

IP-MAT-out: (npr "entity" "mary") "arg0" ((some lc fh "time"
            (nn lc "week")) "for" (embVerb lc "event" ["arg0",
            "for"] "has_been_meaning" (toComp lc (verb lc
            "event" nil "go"))))__LOCAL__"toComp"@NAME@"for"
```

Local binding names additional to defaults `"arg0"`, `"arg1"` and `"h"` are collected on the right side of `__LOCAL__` in the above intermediate results. The resulting list of local names is integrated with `fn lc =>`, together with a list of the distinct fresh binding names included with `fn fh =>`, to make the overall output from conversion as follows:

```
val ex1 =
( fn fh =>
  ( fn lc =>
    ( ( npr "entity" "mary")
      "arg0"
      ( ( some lc fh "time"
          ( nn lc "week"))
        "for"
        ( embVerb lc "event" ["arg0", "for"] "has_been_meaning"
          ( toComp lc
```

```
                 ( verb lc "event" nil "go")))))))
   ["toComp", "for", "arg0", "arg1", "h"])
["constant", "event", "time"]
```

Evaluation is possible when `ex1` is placed under `CClose` collecting values for the `"constant"` name and an existential closure of the `"event"` and `"time"` names:

```
> SctToLang.eval (
    fn _ => nil,
    Sct.CClose ("constant",
      closureEnv "∃" ("ENTITY", "entity") ["event", "time"] ex1));
```

val it =
Quant ("time", ["event", "time"], "∃", [X (1, "time")],
 Quant ("event", ["event", "time"], "∃", [X (3, "event"), X (2, "event")],
 REL ("", [Throw ("time", REL ("week", [At (X (1, "time"), "h")])),
  REL ("has_been_meaning", [At (C ("mary", "entity"), "arg0"),
  At (X (1, "time"), "for"), At (X (3, "event"), "event"),
  At (
  REL ("go", [At (C ("mary", "entity"), "arg0"),
   At (X (2, "event"), "event")]), "toComp")])])))
: Lang.t

With post-processing and pretty printing the evaluation result produces:

$\exists t_1 e_2 e_3$ (week (t_1) $\wedge$ has_been_meaning $(e_3,$ mary, go $(e_2,$ mary)) $\wedge$
  for (e_3) $=$ $t_1)$

Triggered by the IP-INF node of the annotation, `toComp` in `ex1` establishes a control relationship in which the subject of the matrix clause, *mary*, is also the subject of the infinitive embedding (see Sect. 3.3.9 for details). Placement in `ex1` of `"for"` as an expected argument of `embVerb` (together with `"arg0"`) makes the *week* that is t_1 a *for* modifier of the *has_been_meaning* event e_2.

4.4 Passives

To capture passives, `passive` is defined. This calls `pass`, with the x parameter value determined by whether `"arg1"` is assigned the empty sequence. When called, `pass` with `Sct.Lam` relocates to x the frontmost sequence value assigned `"arg0"`, and any sequence content assigned to `"lgs"` (logical subject binding) shifts with `Sct.Clean` to the `"arg0"` name.

```
val passive =
fn e =>
 let
  val pass =
  fn x => fn e =>
```

```
  Sct.Lam ("arg0", x, Sct.Clean (0, ["lgs"], "arg0", e))
in
  Sct.If (fn g: Lang.t Assign.t => null (g "arg1"),
    pass "arg1" e, pass "arg2" e)
end
```

Also required is a means to open an `"lgs"` binding from the logical subject if present, to be accomplished with `arg`. Following clearing with `clean` of the binding name given with parameter x, which is typical when opening a local binding, `arg` shifts to x the first sequence value assigned the binding name given with parameter v.

```
val arg =
fn v => fn x => fn e =>
  clean x (Sct.Lam (v, x, e))
```

In English nearly any semantically transitive or ditransitive verb can be passivised. The passive is formed with the auxiliary verb *be* and the main verb in passive participle form. The agent of the active transitive or ditransitive verb can appear preceded by the preposition *by*. Examples (1b) and (1c) are passives of the ditransitive clause (1a):

(1) a. Brutus gave Caesar a wound.
    b. A wound was given Caesar by Brutus.
    c. Caesar was given a wound by Brutus.

Annotation of passive sentences gives verbs with VAN (= passive participle) part-of-speech information to trigger presence of the `passive` operation. Example (1b) is annotated:

```
(IP-MAT (NP-SBJ (D A)
                (N wound))
        (BED was)
        (VAN given)
        (NP-OB2 (NPR Caesar))
        (PP (P by)
            (NP (NPR Brutus)))
        (NP-LGS *by*)
        (. .))
```

Example (1c) is annotated:

```
(IP-MAT (NP-SBJ (NPR Caesar))
        (BED was)
        (VAN given)
        (NP-OB1 (D a)
                (N wound))
        (PP (P by)
            (NP (NPR Brutus)))
        (NP-LGS *by*)
        (. .))
```

The annotation includes disambiguation information (NP-LGS *by*) to indicate that
by of the immediately preceding sibling marks the logical subject. While not essential
here, such disambiguation is required for an example like *Cyrus was mentioned by
name by Isaiah.*

The annotation for (1b) arrives at ex2 with conversion. passive has placement
immediately above the main predicate, so as to scope under all arguments. With there
being an argument to create a "by" binding, corresponding to the *by* PP phrase of
the annotation, sensitivity to the "by" name is added to the lc parameter. Positioned
immediately below the "by" argument is (arg "by") "lgs". Occurring because
of (NP-LGS *by*), this serves to shift the "by" binding to an "lgs" binding. Once
opened, an "lgs" binding is destined to be reallocated to an "arg0" binding with
passive before the main predicate is reached, and so addition of "lgs" to the lc
parameter is unnecessary.

```
val ex2 =
( fn fh =>
  ( fn lc =>
    ( ( some lc fh "entity"
        ( nn lc "wound"))
      "arg0"
      ( ( npr "entity" "caesar")
        "arg2"
        ( ( npr "entity" "brutus")
          "by"
          ( ( arg "by")
            "lgs"
            ( passive
              ( verb lc "event" ["arg1", "arg2", "arg0"]
                "given")))))))
  ["by", "arg2", "arg0", "arg1", "h"])
["entity", "constant", "event"]
```

Conversion of the annotation for (1c) arrives at ex3.

```
val ex3 =
( fn fh =>
  ( fn lc =>
    ( ( npr "entity" "caesar")
      "arg0"
      ( ( some lc fh "entity"
          ( nn lc "wound"))
        "arg1"
        ( ( npr "entity" "brutus")
          "by"
          ( ( arg "by")
            "lgs"
```

```
                    ( passive
                      ( verb lc "event" ["arg2", "arg1", "arg0"]
                        "given")))))))
    ["by", "arg1", "arg0", "arg2", "h"])
  ["constant", "entity", "event"]
```

The following demonstrates evaluation of ex2, while an equivalent result arises with ex3:

```
> SctToLang.eval (
    fn _ => nil,
    Sct.CClose ("constant",
      closureEnv "∃" ("ENTITY", "entity")
        ["entity", "event"] ex2));
```
val it =
Quant ("entity", ["event", "entity"], "∃", [X (1, "entity")],
 Quant ("event", ["event", "entity"], "∃", [X (2, "event")],
  REL ("", [Throw ("entity", REL ("wound", [At (X (1, "entity"), "h")])),
  REL ("given", [At (X (1, "entity"), "arg1"),
   At (C ("caesar", "entity"), "arg2"), At (C ("brutus", "entity"), "arg0"),
   At (X (2, "event"), "event")])])])))
: Lang.t

With post-processing and pretty printing the evaluation result produces:

$\exists x_1 e_2 (\text{wound}(x_1) \wedge \text{given}(e_2, \text{brutus}, x_1, \text{caesar}))$

Thus, what begins as an NP-SBJ argument of the annotation, as an argument of the converted SCT expression creates an "arg0" binding that shifts with passive to be an object binding, while if an "lgs" binding is opened this becomes the "arg0" binding.

4.5 Adverbial Clauses (CP-ADV)

Methods are required to integrate the content of adverbial clauses as clausal modifiers of a containing clause. This is accomplished in one of three ways. Firstly, with coordination:

```
val coord =
fn fh => fn s => fn e1 => fn e2 =>
 Sct.Rel (fh, map (fn _ => "c") fh, s, [e1, e2])
```

Secondly, with quantified closures to create a conditional encoding:

```
val cond =
fn fh => fn v => fn s => fn e1 => fn e2 =>
 closureEnv "∀" (v, v) fh (
  Sct.Rel (fh, map (fn _ => "c") fh, s, [
   e1,
   closureEnv "∃" (v, v) fh e2]))
```

Thirdly, with someFact to connect clause content, e1, to a binding argument opened
for the rest of the containing clause, e2. Additional parameters for someFact are: fh
to state the fresh bindings; (v, sort), binding name and sort information for the
binding to be created; and x, the name under which the created binding continues in
the containing clause.

```
val someFact =
fn fh => fn (v, sort) => fn e1 => fn x => fn e2 =>
 classic (v, sort) x (
  manage fh [
   Sct.Throw (v,
    rel "fact" [
     Sct.At (Sct.T (x, 0), "fact"),
     Sct.At (Sct.Lam (x, "", e1), "that")]),
   e2])
```

Adverbial clauses in English are normally introduced by one of a special set of
adverbial clause introducers (subordinate conjunctions); notably, *although, because,
if, unless* and *when*. With the annotation system, most adverbial clause introducers
are treated as prepositions, and thus many adverbial clauses are represented as PPs
in which the preposition takes a clausal complement. As an illustration, consider
(2) which allows the distinct readings of (3). The ambiguity hinges on the scope
placement of negation with respect to *because*, with *she* anaphorically dependent on
a collector for both readings.

(2)   A collector didn't buy because she was influenced.

(3) a.   A collector made the purchase, for a reason not yet stated.
         (neg > because)
    b.   For the reason stated, a collector didn't make the purchase.
         (because > neg)

Reading (3a) is captured with the following annotation:

```
(IP-MAT (NP-SBJ (D A)
                (N collector))
        (DOD $did)
        (NEG $n't)
        (VB buy)
        (PP (P+N because)
            (CP-ADV (C 0)
```

```
                        (IP-SUB (NP-SBJ (PRO she))
                                (BED was)
                                (VAN influenced))))
            (CRD *)
            (. .))
```

Presence of CRD (with `(CRD *)`), a tag that is additional to the annotation system, is used to trigger selection of `coord` to integrate the adverbial clause, resulting in ex4. An instance of `subord` ensures there are no bindings from the containing clause for the names of the `lc` parameter inherited by the adverbial clause.

```
val ex4 =
( fn fh =>
  ( fn lc =>
    ( ( some lc fh "entity"
        ( nn lc "collector"))
      "arg0"
      ( neg fh exist
        ( ( coord fh "because"
            ( subord lc nil
              ( ( fn lc =>
                  ( ( pro ["c"] fh ["entity"] ( "entity",
                       "entity") "she")
                    "arg0"
                    ( passive
                      ( verb lc "event" ["arg1"] "influenced"))))
                ["arg0", "arg1", "by", "h"])))
            ( verb lc "event" ["arg0"] "did_buy")))))
  ["arg0", "arg1", "h"])
["entity", "event"]
```

With the annotation maintaining a flat clause structure and with there being no overt scope annotation, linear ordering determines placement of negation outside *because*. In the converted expression the adverbial clause introduced with *because* is incorporated into the overall expression with `coord` having "because" as value for the s parameter, the content of the adverbial clause for e1, and the rest of the containing clause for e2.

The following demonstrates evaluation of ex4:

```
> SctToLang.eval (
    fn _ => nil,
    closureEnv "∃" ("ENTITY", "entity") ["entity", "event"] ex4);
val it =
Quant ("entity", ["event", "entity"], "∃", [X (1, "entity")],
  Quant ("event", ["event", "entity"], "∃", [],
    REL ("", [Throw ("entity", REL ("collector", [At (X (1, "entity"), "h")])]),
      REL ("¬", [
```

Quant ("entity", ["event", "entity"], "∃", [],
Quant ("event", ["event", "entity"], "∃", [X (3, "event"), X (2, "event")],
REL ("because", [
QuantThrow ("entity", X (4, "entity"),
REL ("", [
Throw ("entity",
REL ("she:pick", [X (4, "entity"), X (1, "entity")])),
REL ("influenced", [At (X (4, "entity"), "arg1"),
At (X (2, "event"), "event")])])),
REL ("did_buy", [At (X (1, "entity"), "arg0"),
At (X (3, "event"), "event")])])))])])))
: Lang.t

With post-processing and pretty printing the evaluation result produces:

$\exists x_1$ (collector (x_1) ∧
  ¬ $\exists x_4 e_2 e_3 (x_4 = $ she $\{x_1\}$ ∧
    because (influenced $(e_2, \_, x_4)$, did_buy $(e_3, x_1))))$

The restrictive content contributed by the pronoun of the adverbial clause is relocated with post-processing to the level of existential closure brought about by negation and can be resolved to take *a collector* as its antecedent.

The alternative scope reading of (3b) is captured with annotation that deviates only in -LOW being added to the NEG part-of-speech tag occurring at the clausal level.

```
(IP-MAT (NP-SBJ (D A)
                (N collector))
        (DOD $did)
        (NEG-LOW $n't)
        (VB buy)
        (PP (P+N because)
            (CP-ADV (C 0)
                    (IP-SUB (NP-SBJ (PRO she))
                            (BED was)
                            (VAN influenced))))
        (CRD *)
        (. .))
```

The expression resulting from conversion, ex5, has negation below *because*:

```
val ex5 =
( fn fh =>
  ( fn lc =>
    ( ( some lc fh "entity"
        ( nn lc "collector"))
      "arg0"
      ( ( coord fh "because"
```

```
                  ( subord lc nil
                    ( ( fn lc =>
                        ( ( pro ["c"] fh ["entity"] ( "entity",
                            "entity") "she")
                          "arg0"
                          ( passive
                            ( verb lc "event" ["arg1"] "influenced"))))
                      ["arg0", "arg1", "by", "h"])))
                ( neg fh exist
                  ( verb lc "event" ["arg0"] "did_buy")))))
    ["arg0", "arg1", "h"])
["entity", "event"]
```

The following demonstrates evaluation of ex5:

```
> SctToLang.eval (
    fn _ => nil,
    closureEnv "∃" ("ENTITY", "entity") ["entity", "event"] ex5);
```
val it =
Quant ("entity", ["event", "entity"], "∃", [X (1, "entity")],
 Quant ("event", ["event", "entity"], "∃", [X (2, "event")],
  REL ("", [Throw ("entity", REL ("collector", [At (X (1, "entity"), "h")])),
   REL ("because", [
   QuantThrow ("entity", X (3, "entity"),
    REL ("", [
    Throw ("entity", REL ("she:pick", [X (3, "entity"), X (1, "entity")])),
    REL ("influenced", [At (X (3, "entity"), "arg1"),
     At (X (2, "event"), "event")])])]),
   REL ("¬", [
   Quant ("entity", ["event", "entity"], "∃", [],
   Quant ("event", ["event", "entity"], "∃", [X (4, "event")],
    REL ("did_buy", [At (X (1, "entity"), "arg0"),
     At (X (4, "event"), "event")])))])])])))
: Lang.t

Post-processing relocates to the level of discourse closure the restrictive content of the pronoun of the adverbial clause that can be resolved to take *a collector* as its antecedent:

$$\exists x_3 x_1 e_2 (\text{collector}(x_1) \wedge x_3 = \text{she}\{x_1\} \wedge$$
$$\text{because}(\text{influenced}(e_2, \_, x_3), \neg \exists e_4 \text{did\_buy}(e_4, x_1)))$$

An application of cond is demonstrated with the analysis of (4).

(4) If a collector is influenced she buys.

```
(IP-MAT (PP-HIGH (P If)
              (CP-ADV (C 0)
```

```
                              (IP-SUB (NP-SBJ (D a)
                                              (N collector))
                                      (BEP is)
                                      (VAN influenced))))
              (CND *)
              (NP-SBJ (PRO she))
              (VB buys)
              (. .))
```

Inclusion of tag CND (with `(CND *)`), a tag that like CRD is additional to the annotation system, ensures `cond` integrates the adverbial clause, resulting in ex6. Note
the contribution of the adverbial clause is higher in ex6 than the contribution of the
subject noun phrase *she*. This was determined by annotating PP-HIGH to counter
the influence of the default hierarchy (see Sect. 4.2) where the subject has high
placement.

```
val ex6 =
( fn fh =>
  ( fn lc =>
    ( ( cond fh "entity" "CND_if"
        ( subord lc nil
          ( ( fn lc =>
              ( ( some lc fh "entity"
                  ( nn lc "collector"))
                "arg0"
                ( passive
                  ( verb lc "event" ["arg1"] "influenced"))))
            ["fact", "arg0", "arg1", "by", "h"])))
      ( ( pro ["c"] fh ["entity"] ( "entity", "entity") "she")
        "arg0"
        ( verb lc "event" ["arg0"] "buys"))))
    ["arg0", "arg1", "h"])
  ["entity", "event"]
```

The following demonstrates evaluation of ex6:

```
> SctToLang.eval (
    fn _ => nil,
    closureEnv "∃" ("ENTITY", "entity") ["entity", "event"] ex6);
val it =
Quant ("entity", ["event", "entity"], "∃", [],
 Quant ("event", ["event", "entity"], "∃", [],
  Quant ("entity", ["event", "entity"], "∀", [X (1, "entity")],
   Quant ("event", ["event", "entity"], "∀", [X (2, "event")],
    REL ("CND_if", [
     REL ("", [Throw ("entity", REL ("collector", [At (X (1, "entity"), "h")])),
      REL ("influenced", [At (X (1, "entity"), "arg1"),
```

At (X (2, "event"), "event")])]),
Quant ("entity", ["event", "entity"], "∃", [],
Quant ("event", ["event", "entity"], "∃", [X (3, "event")],
QuantThrow ("entity", X (4, "entity"),
 REL ("", [
 Throw ("entity",
 REL ("she:pick", [X (4, "entity"), X (1, "entity")])),
 REL ("buys", [At (X (4, "entity"), "arg0"),
 At (X (3, "event"), "event")])])))))])))))
: Lang.t

With post-processing and pretty printing the evaluation result produces:

$$\forall x_1 e_2 \text{if} (\text{collector}(x_1) \wedge \text{influenced}(e_2, \_, x_1),$$
$$\exists x_4 e_3 (x_4 = \text{she}\{x_1\} \wedge \text{buys}(e_3, x_4)))$$

Notably *a collector* of the adverbial clause receives universal quantification from the closure brought about by cond and serves as accessible antecedent for the subject pronoun *she* of the matrix clause, illustrating an archetypal donkey anaphora dependency (Kamp 1981).

When annotation contains neither CRD nor CND, the default is for the adverbial clause to integrate with someFact, as can be demonstrated with the analysis of (5).

(5) This is because a collector was influenced.

```
(IP-MAT (NP-SBJ (D This))
        (BEP is)
        (PP (P+N because)
            (CP-ADV (C 0)
                    (IP-SUB (NP-SBJ (D a)
                                    (N collector))
                            (BED was)
                            (VAN influenced)))))
        (. .))
```

Conversion arrives at ex7. The adverbial clause is incorporated with someFact creating a fresh binding of sort "situation" that will take scope with a commanding "situation" closure. This freshly created binding shifts outside the restriction to the "because" binding name and to "" inside the restriction to have no further consequences.

```
val ex7 =
( fn fh =>
  ( fn lc =>
    ( ( pro ["c"] fh ["entity"] ( "entity", "entity") "this")
      "arg0"
      ( ( someFact fh ( "situation", "situation")
          ( subord lc nil
```

```
        ( ( fn lc =>
            ( ( some lc fh "entity"
                ( nn lc "collector"))
              "arg0"
              ( passive
                ( verb lc "event" ["arg1"] "influenced"))))
            ["arg0", "arg1", "by", "h"])))
        "because"
        ( verb lc "event" ["arg0"] "is"))))
  ["because", "arg0", "arg1", "h"])
["entity", "event", "situation"]
```

The following demonstrates evaluation of ex7:

```
> SctToLang.eval (
    fn _ => nil,
    closureEnv "∃" ("ENTITY", "entity")
    ["entity", "event", "situation"] ex7);
```

val it =
Quant ("entity", ["situation", "event", "entity"], "∃", [X (1, "entity")],
Quant ("event", ["situation", "event", "entity"], "∃", [X (3, "event"), X (2, "event")],
Quant ("situation", ["situation", "event", "entity"], "∃", [],
  QuantThrow ("entity", X (4, "entity"),
  REL ("", [Throw ("entity", REL ("this:pick", [X (4, "entity")]))),
  QuantThrow ("situation", X (5, "situation"),
  REL ("", [
   Throw ("situation",
   REL ("fact", [At (X (5, "situation"), "fact"),
   At (
    REL ("", [
    Throw ("entity", REL ("collector", [At (X (1, "entity"), "h")])),
    REL ("influenced", [At (X (1, "entity"), "arg1"),
     At (X (2, "event"), "event")])]), "that")])),
   REL ("is", [At (X (4, "entity"), "arg0"),
   At (X (5, "situation"), "because"),
   At (X (3, "event"), "event")])])))])))))
: Lang.t

With post-processing and pretty printing the evaluation result produces:

$\exists x_4 x_1 e_2 e_3 s_5$ (is_fact_that (s_5, influenced (e_2, _, x_1)) $\wedge$ x_4 = this $\wedge$
   collector (x_1) $\wedge$ is (e_3, x_4) $\wedge$ because (e_3) = s_5)

Here, *because* is an event modifier equated to a situation where the proposition "the collector was influenced" is true. This assumes situations to be in the domain of individuals and for *is_fact_that* to hold as a relation between a situation and the corresponding true proposition, following the 'fact' analysis of Moore (1995) used for the analysis of adverbs in Sect. 4.8.

4.6 Participial Clauses (IP-PPL)

The methods of `coord`, `cond` and `someFact` that integrate the content of adverbial clauses as clausal modifiers can also be used with participial clauses. Like adverbial clauses, participial clauses are subordinate clauses, so integration with a containing clause poses the danger of inheriting unexpected bindings. With adverbial clauses all bindings from the containing clause are removed (to `"c"`) with `subord`. Matters are less straightforward for participial clauses, since typically inheritance of an `"arg0"` binding is required from the containing clause. The possibility of maintaining a single binding for `"arg0"` will be achieved with `control` of Sect. 3.3.9.

Participial clauses in English take non-finite verbs with suffix *-ed* or *-ing* and can either appear with one of a limited set of prepositions (e.g., (6a)), with an adverbial clause introducer (e.g., (6b)), or without an introducer (e.g., (6c)).

(6) a. In jumping a burn I slipped.
   b. I shall drop, unless supported by a Rummer of Wine.
   c. We found Warre in the garden, trampling among the flower-beds.

The participial clause of (6a) is introduced with preposition *in*, and is annotated as follows:

```
(IP-MAT (PP (P In)
            (IP-PPL (VAG jumping)
                    (NP-OB1 (D a)
                            (N burn))))
        (NP-SBJ (PRO I))
        (VBD slipped)
        (. .))
```

Conversion arrives at `ex8`. The participial clause is integrated with `someFact` opening an `"in"` binding for the containing clause, with a placement below the subject and so inside the scope of the `"arg0"` binding, in accordance with the hierarchy of Sect. 4.2.

```
val ex8 =
( fn fh =>
  ( fn lc =>
    ( ( pro ["personalc"] fh ["entity"] ( "ENTITY",
        "personalentity") "i")
      "arg0"
      ( ( someFact fh ( "situation", "situation")
          ( control lc
            ( ( fn lc =>
                ( ( some lc fh "entity"
                    ( nn lc "burn"))
                  "arg1"
                  ( verb lc "event" ["arg1"] "jumping")))
              ["arg1", "arg0", "h"])))
```

```
      "in"
      ( verb lc "event" ["arg0"] "slipped"))))
  ["in", "arg0", "arg1", "h"])
["entity", "event", "situation", "ENTITY"]
```

With evaluation against the empty assignment, of the binding names `"arg0"`, `"arg1"` and `"arg2"`, only a single sequence value is assigned to `"arg0"` with the occurrence of `control` and so it is this binding that is preserved into the participial clause to act as the subject of *jumping*. The following demonstrates evaluation of ex8:

```
> SctToLang.eval (
    fn _ => nil,
    closureEnv "∃" ("ENTITY", "entity")
      ["entity", "event", "situation", "ENTITY"] ex8);
```
val it =
Quant ("ENTITY", ["situation", "event", "entity", "ENTITY"], "∃", [],
 Quant ("entity", ["situation", "event", "entity", "ENTITY"], "∃", [X (1, "entity")],
  Quant ("event", ["situation", "event", "entity", "ENTITY"], "∃", [X (3, "event"), X
(2, "event")],
   Quant ("situation", ["situation", "event", "entity", "ENTITY"], "∃", [],
   QuantThrow ("ENTITY", X (4, "personalentity"),
    REL ("", [Throw ("ENTITY", REL ("i:pick", [X (4, "personalentity")])),
    QuantThrow ("situation", X (5, "situation"),
     REL ("", [
     Throw ("situation",
     REL ("fact", [At (X (5, "situation"), "fact"),
     At (
      REL ("", [Throw ("entity", REL ("burn", [At (X (1, "entity"), "h")])),
       REL ("jumping", [At (X (1, "entity"), "arg1"),
       At (X (4, "personalentity"), "arg0"),
       At (X (2, "event"), "event")])]), "that")])),
      REL ("slipped", [At (X (4, "personalentity"), "arg0"),
      At (X (5, "situation"), "in"), At (X (3, "event"), "event")])])))])))))))
: Lang.t

With post-processing and pretty printing the result from evaluation produces:

$\exists z_4 x_1 e_2 e_3 s_5 (\text{is\_fact\_that}(s_5, \text{jumping}(e_2, z_4, x_1)) \wedge \text{burn}(x_1) \wedge$
$z_4 = \text{i} \wedge \text{slipped}(e_3, z_4) \wedge \text{in}(e_3) = s_5)$

Notably, what is the `"arg0"` binding of the main predicate of the participial clause (*"jumping"*) is the `"arg0"` binding of the main predicate of the containing clause (*"slipped"*).

The participial clause of (6b) is introduced by adverbial clause introducer *unless*. Disambiguation information CND added to the annotation triggers selection of `cond` as the means to integrate the participial clause. Furthermore -LOW scope information ensures low placement for the modal (*shall*).

```
(IP-MAT (NP-SBJ (PRO I))
        (MD-LOW shall)
        (VB drop)
        (, ,)
        (PP (P unless)
            (IP-PPL (VAN supported)
                    (PP (P by)
                        (NP (D a)
                            (N Rummer)
                            (PP (P of)
                                (NP (N Wine)))))
                    (NP-LGS *by*)))
        (CND *)
        (. .))
```

Conversion arrives at ex9, with the participial clause placed below the matrix clause subject and yet above the modal and adverb. As with the previous example, with such placement of the participial clause the "arg0" binding of the containing clause is inherited.

```
val ex9 =
( fn fh =>
  ( fn lc =>
    ( ( pro ["personalc"] fh ["entity"] ( "ENTITY",
        "personalentity") "i")
      "arg0"
      ( ( cond fh "entity" "CND_unless"
          ( control lc
            ( ( fn lc =>
                ( ( some lc fh "entity"
                    ( ( some lc fh "entity"
                        ( nn lc "wine"))
                      "of"
                      ( nn lc "rummer")))
                  "by"
                  ( ( arg "by")
                    "lgs"
                    ( passive
                        ( verb lc "event" ["arg0", "arg1"]
                          "supported")))))
              ["of", "by", "arg1", "arg0", "h"])))
          ( md fh "shall" free
            ( verb lc "event" ["arg0"] "drop")))))
    ["fact", "arg0", "arg1", "h"])
["ENTITY", "entity", "event"]
```

The following demonstrates evaluation of `ex9`:

```
> SctToLang.eval (
    fn _ => nil,
    closureEnv "∃" ("ENTITY", "entity")
     ["ENTITY", "entity", "event"] ex9);
```

val it =
Quant ("ENTITY", ["event", "entity", "ENTITY"], "∃", [],
Quant ("entity", ["event", "entity", "ENTITY"], "∃", [],
* Quant ("event", ["event", "entity", "ENTITY"], "∃", [],*
* QuantThrow ("ENTITY", X (1, "personalentity"),*
* REL ("", [Throw ("ENTITY", REL ("i:pick", [X (1, "personalentity")])]),*
*   Quant ("entity", ["event", "entity"], "∀", [X (3, "entity"), X (2, "entity")],*
*   Quant ("event", ["event", "entity"], "∀", [X (4, "event")],*
*   REL ("CND_unless", [*
*   REL ("", [*
*   Throw ("entity",*
*   REL ("", [Throw ("entity", REL ("wine", [At (X (2, "entity"), "h")])]),*
*   REL ("rummer", [At (X (3, "entity"), "h"),*
*   At (X (2, "entity"), "of")])])]),*
*   REL ("supported", [At (X (3, "entity"), "arg0"),*
*   At (X (1, "personalentity"), "arg1"),*
*   At (X (4, "event"), "event")])]),*
*   Quant ("entity", ["event", "entity"], "∃", [],*
*   Quant ("event", ["event", "entity"], "∃", [X (5, "event")],*
*   REL ("shall", [*
*   REL ("drop", [At (X (1, "personalentity"), "arg0"),*
*   At (X (5, "event"), "event")])])])])))])))])))))*
: Lang.t

Following post-processing and pretty printing the produced result is:

$\exists z_1(z_1 = \text{i} \land$
$\forall x_2 x_3 e_4 \texttt{unless}($
$\quad \text{wine}(x_2) \land \text{is\_rummer\_of}(x_3, x_2) \land \text{supported}(e_4, x_3, z_1),$
$\quad \exists e_5 \text{shall}(\text{drop}(e_5, z_1))))$

Notably, what is, following passivisation, the `"arg1"` binding of the main predicate of the participial clause (*"supported"*) is the `"arg0"` binding of the main predicate of the containing clause (*"drop"*).

Possible annotation for (6c), which has no introducer, is as follows:

```
(IP-MAT (NP-SBJ (PRO We))
        (VBD found)
        (NP-OB1 (NPR Warre))
        (PP (P in)
            (NP (D the)
```

```
                    (N garden))))
         (, ,)
         (IP-PPL (VAG trampling)
                 (PP (P among)
                     (NP (D the)
                         (N+NS flower-beds)))))
         (. .))
```

Conversion arrives at ex10, with the method of incorporating the participial clause
defaulting to the relation of "∧" (conjunction) constructed with coord:

```
val ex10 =
( fn fh =>
  ( fn lc =>
    ( ( pro ["personalc"] fh ["group"] ( "GROUP",
        "personalgroup") "we")
      "arg0"
      ( ( npr "entity" "warre")
        "arg1"
        ( ( some lc fh "ENTITY"
            ( nn lc "garden"))
          "in"
          ( ( coord fh "∧"
              ( control lc
                ( ( fn lc =>
                    ( ( some lc fh "GROUP"
                        ( nn lc "flower-beds"))
                      "among"
                      ( verb lc "event" nil "trampling")))
                    ["among", "arg0", "arg1", "h"])))
              ( verb lc "event" ["arg0", "arg1"] "found")))))))
    ["in", "arg1", "arg0", "h"])
["GROUP", "constant", "ENTITY", "event"]
```

   With evaluation starting from the empty assignment, control in ex10 is placed
into an environment with a single sequence value assigned to "arg0" and a single
sequence value assigned to "arg1". Following control the sequence value assigned
to "arg1" becomes the new frontmost sequence value assigned to "arg0" and so is
preserved into the body of the participial clause as the only sequence value assigned
to "arg0". The following demonstrates an evaluation run with ex10:

```
> SctToLang.eval (
    fn _ => nil,
    Sct.CClose ("constant",
      closureEnv "∃" ("ENTITY", "entity")
      ["GROUP", "constant", "ENTITY", "event"] ex10));
val it =
```

Quant ("ENTITY", ["event", "GROUP", "ENTITY"], "∃", [X (1, "entity")],
 Quant ("GROUP", ["event", "GROUP", "ENTITY"], "∃", [X (2, "group")],
   Quant ("event", ["event", "GROUP", "ENTITY"], "∃", [X (4, "event"), X (3, "event")],
   QuantThrow ("GROUP", X (5, "personalgroup"),
    REL ("", [Throw ("GROUP", REL ("we:pick", [X (5, "personalgroup")])),
    REL ("", [Throw ("ENTITY", REL ("garden", [At (X (1, "entity"), "h")])),
    REL ("∧", [
    REL ("", [Throw ("GROUP", REL ("flower-beds", [At (X (2, "group"), "h")])),
    REL ("trampling", [At (X (2, "group"), "among"),
    At (C ("warre", "entity"), "arg0"), At (X (3, "event"), "event")])]),
    REL ("found", [At (X (5, "personalgroup"), "arg0"),
    At (C ("warre", "entity"), "arg1"), At (X (1, "entity"), "in"),
    At (X (4, "event"), "event")])])])])))))
: Lang.t

Following post-processing and pretty printing the produced result is:

$\exists x_1 Z_5 X_2 e_3 e_4 (Z_5 =$ we $\land$ flower-beds$(X_2) \land$ garden$(x_1) \land$
trampling$(e_3,$ warre$) \land$ among$(e_3) = X_2 \land$
found$(e_4, Z_5,$ warre$) \land$ in$(e_4) = x_1)$

Notably, the `"arg0"` binding of the main predicate of the participial clause (*"trampling"*) is the `"arg1"` binding of the main predicate of the containing clause (*"found"*).

An alternative annotation for (6c) is to mark scope information -HIGH with the participial clause:

```
(IP-MAT (NP-SBJ (PRO We))
        (VBD found)
        (NP-OB1 (NPR Warre))
        (PP (P in)
            (NP (D the)
                (N garden)))
        (, ,)
        (IP-PPL-HIGH (VAG trampling)
                     (PP (P among)
                         (NP (D the)
                             (N+NS flower-beds))))
        (. .))
```

Conversion arrives at `ex11`, with notably the participial clause placed immediately below the scope of the subject (`"arg0"`) binding and outside the scope of the object (`"arg1"`) binding, following the hierarchy of Sect. 4.2:

```
val ex11 =
( fn fh =>
  ( fn lc =>
    ( ( pro ["personalc"] fh ["group"] ( "GROUP",
```

```
                        "personalgroup")  "we")
                "arg0"
                ( ( coord fh "∧"
                    ( control lc
                      ( ( fn lc =>
                          ( ( some lc fh "GROUP"
                              ( nn lc "flower-beds"))
                            "among"
                            ( verb lc "event" nil "trampling")))
                          ["among", "arg0", "arg1", "h"])))
                  ( ( npr "entity" "warre")
                    "arg1"
                    ( ( some lc fh "ENTITY"
                        ( nn lc "garden"))
                      "in"
                      ( verb lc "event" ["arg0", "arg1"] "found"))))))))
    ["in", "arg1", "arg0", "h"])
["GROUP", "constant", "ENTITY", "event"]
```

A pretty print of the post-processed result is as follows:

$$\exists x_1 Z_5 X_2 e_3 e_4 (Z_5 = \text{we} \wedge \text{flower-beds}(X_2) \wedge \text{garden}(x_1) \wedge$$
$$\text{trampling}(e_3, Z_5) \wedge \text{among}(e_3) = X_2 \wedge$$
$$\text{found}(e_4, Z_5, \text{warre}) \wedge \text{in}(e_4) = x_1)$$

Notably, the `"arg0"` binding of the main predicate of the participial clause (*"trampling"*) is the `"arg0"` binding of the main predicate of the containing clause (*"found"*).

4.7 Adjectives

Adjectives without complements are captured with `adj`, while adjectives with complements utilise `embAdj`:

```
val adj =
fn lc => fn s =>
 predicate lc nil nil s

val embAdj =
fn lc => fn s => fn e =>
 predicate lc nil [e] s
```

With these definitions, adjectives bring about predicates without explicit requirements for arguments. Rather arguments are created with `predicate` (see Sect. 3.3.2) determined by whether bindings for names of the `lc` parameter are open. Consequently, argument selection for adjectives is determined by distribution.

Distributionally, adjectives in English function:

1. to modify noun phrases,
2. as attributive predicates either of a small clause or with the copular verb, or
3. as secondary predicates.

Semantically, adjectives express property concepts, such as quality, propensity, colour, etc. Example (7) illustrates *inventive* functioning as a descriptive modifier, and *delightful* as an attributive predicate.

(7) John's inventive examples are delightful.

Example (7) is annotated:

```
(IP-MAT (NP-SBJ (NPR$ John's)
                (ADJ inventive)
                (NS examples))
        (BEP are)
        (ADJP (ADJ delightful))
        (. .))
```

Conversion arrives at ex12:

```
val ex12 =
( fn fh =>
  ( fn lc =>
    ( ( some lc fh "group"
        ( ( npr "entity" "john")
          "of"
          ( ( coord fh "∧"
              ( subord lc ["h"]
                ( adj lc "inventive")))
            ( nn lc "examples")))))
      "arg0"
      ( ( someClassic lc fh ( "attrib", "attrib") nil
          ( adj lc "delightful"))
        "attribute"
        ( verb lc "event" ["arg0", "attribute"] "are"))))
  ["attribute", "of", "arg0", "arg1", "h"])
["constant", "group", "event", "attrib"]
```

Because of subord (see Sect. 3.3.8), the adjective internal to the noun phrase, adj lc "inventive", has placement within an environment where the only open local binding is the noun phrase internal "h"; with notably the "of" binding shifting to "c". adj lc "delightful" is in the restriction of someClassic (see Sect. 3.3.3) where the only local binding is an "h" binding.

The following demonstrates evaluation of `ex12`:

```
> SctToLang.eval (
    fn _ => nil,
    Sct.CClose ("constant",
     closureEnv "∃" ("ENTITY", "entity")
      ["group", "event", "attrib"] ex12));
```

val it =
Quant ("group", ["event", "attrib", "group"], "∃", [X (1, "group")],
 Quant ("attrib", ["event", "attrib", "group"], "∃", [],
 Quant ("event", ["event", "attrib", "group"], "∃", [X (2, "event")],
 REL ("", [
 Throw ("group",
 REL ("∧", [REL ("inventive", [At (X (1, "group"), "h")]),
 REL ("examples", [At (X (1, "group"), "h"),
  At (C ("john", "entity"), "of")])])),
 QuantThrow ("attrib", X (3, "attrib"),
 REL ("", [Throw ("attrib", REL ("delightful", [At (X (3, "attrib"), "h")])),
 REL ("are", [At (X (1, "group"), "arg0"),
  At (X (3, "attrib"), "attribute"), At (X (2, "event"), "event")])])))])))))
: Lang.t

Post-processing and pretty printing the evaluation result produces:

$\exists X_1 A_3 e_2$ (delightful (A_3) $\wedge$ inventive (X_1) $\wedge$ is_examples_of $(X_1,$ john) $\wedge$
   are $(e_2, X_1, A_3))$

With this encoding *inventive*, which serves as a descriptive modifier internally to the noun phrase restriction, is realised as a predicate whose single argument, X_1, is the binding created by the containing noun phrase. As the main attributive predicate of the clause, *delightful* has its single argument, A_3, linked with the `"attribute"` grammatical role to the local `"arg0"` binding by the copular, *are*, which additionally takes an event binding.

The dash tag -SPR, mnemonic for 'secondary predicate', is appended to all clause-level ADJPs that are not attribute predicates either of a small clause or with the copular verb, or labelled ADJP-LOC. Relevant adjectives are illustrated with (8).

(8) a. This keeps them attentive.
     b. He had done it alone.

Example (8a) is annotated:

```
(IP-MAT (NP-SBJ (D This))
        (VBP keeps)
        (NP-OB1 (PRO them))
        (ADJP-SPR (ADJ attentive))
        (. .))
```

Conversion arrives at ex13, with ADJP-SPR taken to trigger choice of coord fh "∧" as the means to integrate the content of the adjective phrase with the clause. The content of the adjective phrase is moreover placed inside control. As a consequence, a single core argument binding from the containing clause is able to remain open inside the adjective phrase under the "arg0" name, and so provide a binding for the adjective.

```
val ex13 =
( fn fh =>
  ( fn lc =>
    ( ( pro ["c"] fh ["entity"] ( "entity", "entity") "this")
      "arg0"
      ( ( pro ["c"] fh ["group"] ( "group", "group") "them")
        "arg1"
        ( ( coord fh "∧"
            ( control lc
              ( adj lc "attentive")))
            ( verb lc "event" ["arg0", "arg1"] "keeps")))))
  ["as", "arg1", "arg0", "h"])
["entity", "group", "event"]
```

The following demonstrates evaluation of ex13:

```
> SctToLang.eval (
    fn _ => nil,
    closureEnv "∃" ("ENTITY", "entity")
    ["entity", "group", "event"] ex13);
```

val it =
Quant ("entity", ["event", "group", "entity"], "∃", [],
Quant ("group", ["event", "group", "entity"], "∃", [],
 Quant ("event", ["event", "group", "entity"], "∃", [X (1, "event")],
 QuantThrow ("entity", X (2, "entity"),
  REL ("", [Throw ("entity", REL ("this:pick", [X (2, "entity")])]),
  QuantThrow ("group", X (3, "group"),
   REL ("", [Throw ("group", REL ("them:pick", [X (3, "group")])]),
    REL ("∧", [REL ("attentive", [At (X (3, "group"), "arg0")]),
    REL ("keeps", [At (X (2, "entity"), "arg0"), At (X (3, "group"), "arg1"),
     At (X (1, "event"), "event")])])])])])))))
: Lang.t

With post-processing and pretty printing the evaluation result produces:

$\exists x_2 X_3 e_1 (X_3 = \text{them} \land x_2 = \text{this} \land \text{attentive}(X_3) \land \text{keeps}(e_1, x_2, X_3))$

Notably, the "arg1" binding of the main predicate (*"keeps"*) is the sole binding of the adjective predicate (*"attentive"*).

Example (8b) is annotated:

```
(IP-MAT (NP-SBJ (PRO He))
        (HVD had)
        (DON done)
        (NP-OB1 (PRO it))
        (ADJP-SPR-HIGH (ADJ alone))
        (. .))
```

Conversion arrives at ex14:

```
val ex14 =
( fn fh =>
  ( fn lc =>
    ( ( pro ["c"] fh ["entity"] ( "entity", "entity") "he")
      "arg0"
      ( ( coord fh "∧"
          ( control lc
            ( adj lc "alone")))
          ( ( pro ["c"] fh ["entity"] ( "entity", "entity") "it")
            "arg1"
            ( verb lc "event" ["arg0", "arg1"] "had_done")))))
  ["arg1", "as", "arg0", "h"])
["entity", "event"]
```

The following demonstrates evaluation of ex14:

```
> SctToLang.eval (
    fn _ => nil,
    closureEnv "∃" ("ENTITY", "entity") ["entity", "event"] ex14);
```
val it =
Quant ("entity", ["event", "entity"], "∃", [],
 Quant ("event", ["event", "entity"], "∃", [X (1, "event")],
  QuantThrow ("entity", X (2, "entity"),
   REL ("", [Throw ("entity", REL ("he:pick", [X (2, "entity")])]),
    REL ("∧", [REL ("alone", [At (X (2, "entity"), "arg0")]),
     QuantThrow ("entity", X (3, "entity"),
      REL ("", [Throw ("entity", REL ("it:pick", [X (3, "entity")])]),
       REL ("had_done", [At (X (2, "entity"), "arg0"),
        At (X (3, "entity"), "arg1"), At (X (1, "event"), "event")])])])])])])))
: Lang.t

With post-processing and pretty printing the evaluation result produces:

$$\exists x_3 x_2 e_1 (x_2 = \text{he} \land x_3 = \text{it} \land \text{alone}(x_2) \land \text{had\_done}(e_1, x_2, x_3))$$

Notably, the "arg0" binding of the main predicate (*"had_done"*) is the sole binding of the adjective predicate (*"alone"*).

4.8 Adverbs

Definitions for adverbs can follow adjectives, with arguments selected by distribution:

```
val adv =
fn lc => fn s =>
 predicate lc nil nil s

val embAdv =
fn lc => fn s => fn e =>
 predicate lc nil [e] s
```

Supporting environments for adverbs are created with `advp`, where `e1` is the content of the adverb phrase and `e2` is the rest of the containing clause.

```
val advp =
fn lc => fn fh => fn event => fn e1 => fn e2 =>
 Sct.If (
   fn g: Lang.t Assign.t => length (g event) = 1
   andalso Sct.count (event, e1) = 0,
   Sct.Copy (event, "fact",
    manage fh [
     Sct.Throw (event, subord lc ["fact"] e1),
     Sct.Lam ("fact", "", e2)]),
   classic (event, "situation") "fact" (
    manage fh [
     Sct.Throw (event, subord lc ["fact"] e1),
     rel "fact" [
      Sct.At (Sct.T ("fact", 0), "fact"),
      Sct.At (Sct.Lam ("fact", "", e2), "that")]])))
```

If there is a single `event` binding when `advp` is called and no support for `event` bindings is required by the content of the adverb phrase (`e1`) (that is, `Sct.count (event, e1)` $= 0$) then the content of the adverb phrase is a modifier of the single open `event` binding, which is copied to a `"fact"` binding. Otherwise the content of the adverb phrase (`e1`) and containing clause (`e2`) are integrated following the 'fact' analysis of Moore (1995). As with the uses of `someFact` in Sects. 4.5 and 4.6, this analysis assumes situations to be in the domain of individuals and for *is_fact_that* to hold as a relation between a situation and the corresponding true proposition.

Adverbs in English are typically defined negatively as the class of content words that have none of the morphosyntactic or distributional properties of nouns, verbs or adjectives (see e.g., Huddleston and Pullum (2002) for additional limits on category membership). Semantically, adverbs express manner, time, location, and a few other notions. Consider (9), which allows distinct readings in which either (10a) obtains (with negation scoping over 'touch Bob deliberately'), or (10b) obtains (with negation scoping over 'touch Bob')

(9) John didn't touch Bob deliberately.

(10) a. John may have touched Bob, but any contact is accidental.
(neg > deliberately)
b. John does not touch Bob and his restraint is premeditated.
(deliberately > neg)

The following annotation captures reading (10a):

```
(IP-MAT (NP-SBJ (NPR John))
        (DOD $did)
        (NEG $n't)
        (VB touch)
        (NP-OB1 (NPR Bob))
        (ADVP (ADV deliberately))
        (. .))
```

Conversion arrives at ex15, with advp creating an environment to support the adverb:

```
val ex15 =
( fn fh =>
  ( fn lc =>
    ( ( npr "entity" "john")
      "arg0"
      ( neg fh exist
        ( ( npr "entity" "bob")
          "arg1"
          ( ( advp lc fh "event"
              ( adv lc "deliberately"))
            ( verb lc "event" ["arg0", "arg1"] "did_touch")))))))
    ["fact", "arg1", "arg0", "h"])
["constant", "event"]
```

The following demonstrates evaluation of ex15:

```
> SctToLang.eval (
    fn _ => nil,
    Sct.CClose ("constant",
      closureEnv "∃" ("ENTITY", "entity") ["event"] ex15));
```
val it =
Quant ("event", ["event"], "∃", [],
REL ("¬", [
Quant ("event", ["event"], "∃", [X (1, "event")],
REL ("", [Throw ("event", REL ("deliberately", [At (X (1, "event"), "fact")])),
REL ("did_touch", [At (C ("john", "entity"), "arg0"),
At (C ("bob", "entity"), "arg1"), At (X (1, "event"), "event")])])])])
: Lang.t

With post-processing and pretty printing the evaluation result produces:

$\neg\ \exists e_1\,(\text{deliberately}\,(e_1)\ \wedge\ \text{did\_touch}\,(e_1,\ \text{john},\ \text{bob}))$

This follows the standard Davidsonian analysis (Davidson 1967) of treating adverbs as making additional predications of the event binding of the containing clause.

Reading (10b) is obtained with the following annotation that deviates only in -HIGH being added to the ADVP phrasal tag occurring at the clausal level.

```
(IP-MAT (NP-SBJ (NPR John))
        (DOD $did)
        (NEG $n't)
        (VB touch)
        (NP-OB1 (NPR Bob))
        (ADVP-HIGH (ADV deliberately))
        (. .))
```

Conversion arrives at ex16, conforming to the scope hierarchy of Sect. 4.2 with the high placement of advp creating an environment to support the adverb:

```
val ex16 =
( fn fh =>
  ( fn lc =>
    ( ( advp lc fh "event"
        ( adv lc "deliberately"))
      ( ( npr "entity" "john")
        "arg0"
        ( neg fh exist
          ( ( npr "entity" "bob")
            "arg1"
            ( verb lc "event" ["arg0", "arg1"] "did_touch"))))))
  ["arg1", "arg0", "fact", "h"])
["constant", "event"]
```

The following demonstrates evaluation of ex16:

```
> SctToLang.eval (
    fn _ => nil,
    Sct.CClose ("constant",
    closureEnv "∃" ("ENTITY", "entity") ["event"] ex16));
```
val it =
Quant ("event", ["event"], "∃", [],
QuantThrow ("event", X (1, "situation"),
REL ("", [
Throw ("event", REL ("deliberately", [At (X (1, "situation"), "fact")])),
REL ("fact", [At (X (1, "situation"), "fact"),
At (
REL ("¬", [

Quant ("event", ["event"], "∃", [X (2, "event")],
* REL ("did_touch", [At (C ("john", "entity"), "arg0"),*
* At (C ("bob", "entity"), "arg1"), At (X (2, "event"), "event")]))]),*
* "that")])])))*
: Lang.t

With post-processing and pretty printing the evaluation result produces:

$\exists s_1$ (deliberately (s_1) ∧ is_fact_that $(s_1,$ ¬ $\exists e_2$ did_touch $(e_2,$ john, bob)))

This says there exists a situation of there being no event of touching-by-John-of-Bob and this was deliberately so, or more informally, the situation of John not touching Bob was deliberate.

4.9 Floating Quantifiers

This section provides a handle on the phenomenon of 'quantifier float' (see e.g., Payne 2010) with floatingQuantifier:

```
val floatingQuantifier =
fn fh => fn (v, sort) => fn oper => fn x => fn e =>
 closeAll oper [(v, sort)] (
  Sct.Use (v,
   rel "" [
    rel "" [
     Sct.At (Sct.T (v, 0), "h"),
     Sct.At (Sct.T (x, 0), "of")],
    Sct.Lam (x, "",
    Sct.Lam (v, x, closureEnv "∃" (v, sort) fh e))]))
```

With (v, sort) closures, floatingQuantifier brings about an instance of oper quantification that is restricted to be related to the open x binding. The open x binding is subsequently removed from having a further binding role (with a shift to " "), while the newly created quantified value shifts to form a new x binding, essentially replacing the initial x binding. Following post-processing, the restriction of the new x binding to the initial x binding will arise as an "is_of" relation, the fully specified meaning of which depends on the sorts of the related values following Table 4.1.

Table 4.1 "is_of" meanings

x sort	y sort	x "is_of" y meaning
"entity"	"entity"	$=$
"entity"	"group"	$\in$
"group"	"group"	$\subseteq$

Quantifier float from an object is possible when there is another element that follows, as seen with (11).

(11) We gave the boys only a shilling. (cf. We gave only the boys a shilling.)

With BIND to specify the binding to which the floating quantifier applies, example (11) is annotated:

```
(IP-MAT (NP-SBJ (PRO We))
        (VBD gave)
        (NP-OB2 (D the)
                (NS boys))
        (Q only)
        (BIND *arg2*)
        (NP-OB1 (D a)
                (N shilling))
        (. .))
```

Conversion arrives at ex17.

```
val ex17 =
( fn fh =>
  ( fn lc =>
    ( ( pro ["personalc"] fh ["group"] ( "GROUP",
        "personalgroup") "we")
      "arg0"
      ( ( some lc fh "GROUP"
          ( nn lc "boys"))
        "arg2"
        ( ( floatingQuantifier fh ( "entity", "entity") "ONLY")
          "arg2"
          ( ( some lc fh "entity"
              ( nn lc "shilling"))
            "arg1"
            ( verb lc "event" ["arg0", "arg2", "arg1"]
              "gave")))))))
  ["arg1", "arg2", "arg0", "h"])
["GROUP", "entity", "event"]
```

The following demonstrates evaluation of ex17:

```
> SctToLang.eval (
    fn _ => nil,
    closureEnv "∃" ("ENTITY", "entity")
    ["entity", "GROUP", "event"] ex17);
val it =
Quant ("GROUP", ["event", "entity", "GROUP"], "∃", [X (1, "group")],
 Quant ("entity", ["event", "entity", "GROUP"], "∃", [],
```

Quant ("event", ["event", "entity", "GROUP"], "∃", [],
QuantThrow ("GROUP", X (2, "personalgroup"),
 REL ("", [Throw ("GROUP", REL ("we:pick", [X (2, "personalgroup")])]),
  REL ("", [Throw ("GROUP", REL ("boys", [At (X (1, "group"), "h")])]),
  Quant ("entity", ["entity"], "ONLY", [X (3, "entity")],
   REL ("", [REL ("", [At (X (3, "entity"), "h"), At (X (1, "group"), "of")]),
   Quant ("entity", ["event", "entity"], "∃", [X (4, "entity")],
   Quant ("event", ["event", "entity"], "∃", [X (5, "event")],
    REL ("", [
    Throw ("entity", REL ("shilling", [At (X (4, "entity"), "h")])),
    REL ("gave", [At (X (2, "personalgroup"), "arg0"),
    At (X (3, "entity"), "arg2"), At (X (4, "entity"), "arg1"),
    At (X (5, "event"), "event")])])))])])])))))
: Lang.t

With post-processing and pretty printing the evaluation result produces:

$\exists Z_2 X_1 (Z_2 = \text{we} \land \text{boys}(X_1) \land$
$\text{ONLY}x_3 (x_3 \in X_1, \exists x_4 e_5 (\text{shilling}(x_4) \land \text{gave}(e_5, Z_2, x_4, x_3))))$

That is, only members of the group of boys X_1 are given a shilling by Z_2.

4.10 Pronominal Binding and Covaluation

Examples of this section and the next rely on `focusParticle` to capture *only* as a focus particle:

```
val focusParticle =
fn fh => fn (v, sort) => fn oper => fn e1 => fn x => fn e2 =>
 e1 x (floatingQuantifier fh (v, sort) oper x e2)
```

Consider the data of (12) from Partee (1975) and Higginbotham (1980) (see also Bouchard 1985). Example (12a) is unambiguous: it asserts that John and John alone has expectations of winning, that is, a bound interpretation. Example (12b) is without a bound interpretation like (12a) but does admit a covaluation interpretation under which *him* and *John* are coincidentally coreferential so that John and John alone expects John to win; with the others expecting someone other than John to win, if they have expectations. Among its readings, (12c) admits both a bound interpretation equivalent to (12a), and an interpretation equivalent to the covaluation interpretation of (12b). That is, by occurring in an embedded clause, a pronoun maintains the option of a covaluation interpretation, while also creating the option of a bound interpretation.

(12) a. Only John expects himself to win.
     b. Only John expects him to win.
     c. Only John expects that he will win.

Example (12a) is annotated as follows:

```
(IP-MAT (NP-SBJ (FP Only)
                (NPR John))
        (VBP expects)
        (NP-OB1 (PRO himself))
        (IP-INF (TO to)
                (VB win))
        (. .))
```

Conversion arrives at ex18. For the encoding of the reflexive *himself*, the lc parameter, which lists the possible local bindings, is used to specify the sources for
antecedents. Note that the local binding name used to create the reflexive binding itself is removed from the lc parameter internally to the definition of pro (see
Sect. 3.3.6).

```
val ex18 =
( fn fh =>
  ( fn lc =>
    ( ( focusParticle fh ( "entity", "entity") "ONLY"
        ( npr "entity" "john"))
      "arg0"
      ( ( pro lc fh ["entity"] ( "entity", "entity") "himself")
        "arg1"
        ( embVerb lc "event" ["arg0", "arg1"] "expects"
          ( toComp lc
            ( verb lc "event" nil "win"))))))
  ["toComp", "arg1", "arg0", "h"])
["constant", "entity", "event"]
```

The following demonstrates evaluation of ex18:

```
> SctToLang.eval (
    fn "c" => [Lang.C ("John", "entity")]
     | _ => nil,
    Sct.CClose ("constant",
    closureEnv "∃" ("ENTITY", "entity")
      ["entity", "event"] ex18));
```
val it =
Quant ("entity", ["event", "entity"], "∃", [],
 Quant ("event", ["event", "entity"], "∃", [],
  Quant ("entity", ["entity"], "ONLY", [X (1, "entity")],
   REL ("", [
   REL ("", [At (X (1, "entity"), "h"), At (C ("john", "entity"), "of")]),
    Quant ("entity", ["event", "entity"], "∃", [],
     Quant ("event", ["event", "entity"], "∃", [X (3, "event"), X (2, "event")],
      QuantThrow ("entity", X (4, "entity"),

```
REL ("", [
  Throw ("entity",
  REL ("himself:pick", [X (4, "entity"), X (1, "entity")])),
  REL ("expects", [At (X (1, "entity"), "arg0"),
  At (X (4, "entity"), "arg1"), At (X (3, "event"), "event"),
  At (
    REL ("win", [At (X (4, "entity"), "arg0"),
    At (X (2, "event"), "event")]), "toComp")])]))))])))))
: Lang.t
```

With post-processing and pretty printing the evaluation result produces:

$ONLY x_1 (x_1 = john,$
$\exists x_4 e_2 e_3 (x_4 = himself\{x_1\} \wedge expects(e_3, x_1, x_4, win(e_2, x_4))))$

Contributed by *himself*, x_4 has the x_1 binding created by *Only John* as its only potential antecedent, resulting in an unambiguous bound interpretation.

Example (12b) is annotated as follows:

```
(IP-MAT (NP-SBJ (FP Only)
                (NPR John))
        (VBP expects)
        (NP-OB1 (PRO him))
        (IP-INF (TO to)
                (VB win))
        (. .))
```

Conversion arrives at ex19:

```
val ex19 =
( fn fh =>
  ( fn lc =>
    ( ( focusParticle fh ( "entity", "entity") "ONLY"
        ( npr "entity" "john"))
      "arg0"
      ( ( pro ["c"] fh ["entity"] ( "entity", "entity") "him")
        "arg1"
        ( embVerb lc "event" ["arg0", "arg1"] "expects"
          ( toComp lc
            ( verb lc "event" nil "win")))))))
  ["toComp", "arg1", "arg0", "h"])
["constant", "entity", "event"]
```

The following demonstrates evaluation of ex19:

```
> SctToLang.eval (
    fn "c" => [Lang.C ("John", "entity")]
     | _ => nil,
    Sct.CClose ("constant",
```

```
      closureEnv "∃" ("ENTITY", "entity")
      ["entity", "event"] ex19));
```
val it =
Quant ("entity", ["event", "entity"], "∃", [],
Quant ("event", ["event", "entity"], "∃", [],
 Quant ("entity", ["entity"], "ONLY", [X (1, "entity")],
  REL ("", [
  REL ("", [At (X (1, "entity"), "h"), At (C ("john", "entity"), "of")]),
  Quant ("entity", ["event", "entity"], "∃", [],
   Quant ("event", ["event", "entity"], "∃", [X (3, "event"), X (2, "event")],
   QuantThrow ("entity", X (4, "entity"),
    REL ("", [
    Throw ("entity",
    REL ("him:pick", [X (4, "entity"), C ("john", "entity")])),
    REL ("expects", [At (X (1, "entity"), "arg0"),
    At (X (4, "entity"), "arg1"), At (X (3, "event"), "event"),
    At (
     REL ("win", [At (X (4, "entity"), "arg0"),
     At (X (2, "event"), "event")]), "toComp")])])))])))
: Lang.t

With post-processing and pretty printing the evaluation result produces:

ONLYx_1 (x_1 = john,
$\exists x_4 e_2 e_3$ (x_4 = him{john} $\wedge$ expects(e_3, x_1, x_4, win(e_2, x_4))))

In contrast to *himself* from (12a) in ex18, *him* from (12b) in ex19 is unable to link to the local binding of *Only John* but may instead link to 'john' for a covaluation interpretation, where 'john' is a sequence element assigned "c" with the initial state of the assignment.

    Example (12c) is annotated as follows:

```
(IP-MAT (NP-SBJ (FP Only)
                (NPR John))
        (VBP expects)
        (CP-THT (C that)
                (IP-SUB (NP-SBJ (PRO he))
                        (MD will)
                        (VB win)))
        (. .))
```

Conversion arrives at ex20:

```
val ex20 =
( fn fh =>
  ( fn lc =>
    ( ( focusParticle fh ( "entity", "entity") "ONLY"
        ( npr "entity" "john"))
```

```
              "arg0"
            ( embVerb lc "event" ["arg0"] "expects"
              ( that lc
                ( ( pro ["c"] fh ["entity"] ( "entity", "entity") "he")
                  "arg0"
                  ( md fh "will" free
                    ( verb lc "event" ["arg0"] "win")))))))
    ["arg0", "that", "arg1", "h"])
["constant", "entity", "event"]
```

The following demonstrates evaluation of ex20:

```
> SctToLang.eval (
    fn "c" => [Lang.C ("John", "entity")]
     | _ => nil,
    Sct.CClose ("constant",
     closureEnv "∃" ("ENTITY", "entity")
       ["entity", "event"] ex20));
```

val it =
Quant ("entity", ["event", "entity"], "∃", [],
 Quant ("event", ["event", "entity"], "∃", [],
  Quant ("entity", ["entity"], "ONLY", [X (1, "entity")],
   REL ("", [
   REL ("", [At (X (1, "entity"), "h"), At (C ("john", "entity"), "of")]),
   Quant ("entity", ["event", "entity"], "∃", [],
    Quant ("event", ["event", "entity"], "∃", [X (3, "event"), X (2, "event")],
    REL ("expects", [At (X (1, "entity"), "arg0"),
     At (X (3, "event"), "event"),
     At (
      QuantThrow ("entity", X (4, "entity"),
       REL ("", [
       Throw ("entity",
        REL ("he:pick", [X (4, "entity"), X (1, "entity"),
        C ("john", "entity")])),
       REL ("will", [
        REL ("win", [At (X (4, "entity"), "arg0"),
        At (X (2, "event"), "event")])])]))), "that")])])))
: Lang.t

After post-processing and pretty printing the evaluation result produces:

$ONLYx_1 (x_1 = john,$
$\exists x_4 e_2 e_3 (x_4 = he\{x_1, john\} \wedge expects(e_3, x_1, will(win(e_2, x_4)))))$

With its embedded placement, *him* from (12c) in ex20 can take as antecedent either the binding from *Only John* or 'john' present with the initial assignment state. This demonstrates how ambiguity between binding and covaluation readings can arise when there is sufficient embedding.

4.11 Binding and Covaluation with Quantification

Heim (1993) observes that the ambiguity illustrated with (12c) is also found when the antecedent is not referential. In particular the ambiguity can show up under quantification. Thus (13) has the possibility of being construed either with a bound reading where every wife has the thought 'No one else respects their own husband!', or with a covaluation reading where every wife has the thought 'No one else respects my husband!'.

(13)   Every wife thinks that only she respects her husband.

Example (13) is annotated:

```
(IP-MAT (NP-SBJ (Q Every)
                (N wife))
        (VBP thinks)
        (CP-THT (C that)
                (IP-SUB (NP-SBJ (FP only)
                                (PRO she))
                        (VBP respects)
                        (NP-OB1 (PRO$ her)
                                (N husband))))
        (. .))
```

Conversion arrives at ex21:

```
val ex21 =
( fn fh =>
  ( fn lc =>
    ( ( every lc fh ( "entity", "entity")
        ( nn lc "wife"))
      "arg0"
      ( embVerb lc "event" ["arg0"] "thinks"
        ( that lc
          ( ( focusParticle fh ( "entity", "entity") "ONLY"
              ( pro ["c"] fh ["entity"] ( "entity", "entity")
                "she"))
            "arg0"
            ( ( some lc fh "entity"
                ( ( pro ["c"] fh ["entity"] ( "entity",
                      "entity") "her")
                  "of"
                  ( nn lc "husband")))
              "arg1"
              ( verb lc "event" ["arg0", "arg1"]
                "respects"))))))))
```

```
    ["of", "arg1", "arg0", "that", "h"])
  ["entity", "event"]
```

The following demonstrates evaluation of ex21:

```
> SctToLang.eval (
    fn _ => nil,
    closureEnv "∃" ("ENTITY", "entity") ["entity", "event"] ex21);
val it =
```
Quant ("entity", ["event", "entity"], "∃", [],
 Quant ("event", ["event", "entity"], "∃", [],
  Quant ("entity", ["event", "entity"], "∀", [X (1, "entity")],
   Quant ("event", ["event", "entity"], "∀", [],
    REL ("", [Throw ("entity", REL ("wife", [At (X (1, "entity"), "h")]))),
     Quant ("entity", ["event", "entity"], "∃", [],
      Quant ("event", ["event", "entity"], "∃", [X (2, "event")],
       REL ("thinks", [At (X (1, "entity"), "arg0"),
       At (X (2, "event"), "event"),
       At (
        QuantThrow ("entity", X (3, "entity"),
         REL ("", [
          Throw ("entity",
           REL ("she:pick", [X (3, "entity"), X (1, "entity")])),
           Quant ("entity", ["entity"], "ONLY", [X (4, "entity")],
           REL ("", [
            REL ("", [At (X (4, "entity"), "h"), At (X (3, "entity"), "of")]),
             Quant ("entity", ["event", "entity"], "∃", [X (5, "entity")],
              Quant ("event", ["event", "entity"], "∃", [X (6, "event")],
               REL ("", [
                Throw ("entity",
                QuantThrow ("entity", X (7, "entity"),
                 REL ("", [
                  Throw ("entity",
                   REL ("her:pick", [X (7, "entity"), X (4, "entity"),
                   X (1, "entity")])),
                   REL ("husband", [At (X (5, "entity"), "h"),
                    At (X (7, "entity"), "of")])])))),
                 REL ("respects", [At (X (4, "entity"), "arg0"),
                 At (X (5, "entity"), "arg1"),
                 At (X (6, "event"), "event")])])))])]), "that")])))])))))
: Lang.t

With post-processing and pretty printing the evaluation result produces:

$\forall x_1 (\text{wife}(x_1) \rightarrow$
  $\exists x_3 e_2 (x_3 = \text{she}\{x_1\} \wedge$
    $\text{thinks}(e_2, x_1,$
      $\text{ONLY} x_4 (x_4 = x_3,$
        $\exists x_7 x_5 e_6 (x_7 = \text{her}\{x_4, x_1\} \wedge \text{is\_husband\_of}(x_5, x_7) \wedge$
          $\text{respects}(e_6, x_4, x_5)))))))$

While x_3 should be resolved to take x_1 as antecedent, for x_7 there is choice: resolving to x_4 results in the bound reading, while resolving to x_1 brings about the covaluation reading.

4.12 Wh-Questions (CP-QUE)

A question prompts presence of `question` in the converted SCT expression to introduce question operator `"QUEST"`, as well as a `"qentity"` closure with '?' to capture bindings under question. Also, there is `basic` existential closure with `exist` (see Sect. 3.3.4).

```
val question =
fn fh => fn e =>
 rel "QUEST" [
  closureEnv "?" ("qentity", "entity") fh (exist fh e)]
```

A displaced wh-noun phrase will open a binding for a name that is neither fresh nor local (that is, distinct from the names of the `fh` and `lc` parameters). This creates the need to reallocate to a local binding name the binding opened by the displaced wh-phrase if the wh-phrase is to have a binding consequence. Such integration can be achieved with `arg` of Sect. 4.4 bringing about the end of the wh-dependency and the beginning of a local dependency that with sufficient embedding will further shift to a context binding.

With the annotation system both indirect and direct questions are labelled CP-QUE. All indirect questions are treated as having both a wh-position and a complementiser position. Both positions are always shown, whether filled or empty (except for infinitival questions that have no C position). In Modern English the complementiser position of indirect questions is always empty, represented by 0, but could be filled in Middle English (e.g., *Mary asked what time that Jane was coming*).

```
(CP-QUE (WNP (WPRO who))                INDIRECT QUESTION
        (C 0)
        (IP-SUB ...))
```

In contrast to indirect questions, direct questions have only a wh-position at the CP level. The complementiser position in direct questions is generally assumed to be filled by the tensed verb, but this is not represented with the annotation system; rather, no complementiser position is included and the verb is first in the IP-SUB complement (following the trace if there is one). This applies to all constructions in which the verb is clearly in C, including yes/no questions and verb-first conditionals.

```
(CP-QUE (WNP (WPRO what))          DIRECT QUESTION
        (IP-SUB ...))
```

Within the IP-SUB complement, a trace is the first element unless it is contained within a lower constituent, such as a PP within the IP-SUB.

As an example of an indirect question, consider:

(14) You can judge what works.

Example (14) is annotated:

```
(IP-MAT (NP-SBJ (PRO You))
        (MD can)
        (VB judge)
        (CP-QUE (WNP-1 (WPRO what))
                (C 0)
                (IP-SUB (NP-SBJ *T*-1)
                        (VBP works)))
        (. .))
```

Conversion arrives at ex22. The annotation system prescribes coindexing the trace and associated wh-constituent. The coindexing of the annotation, "-1", reaches the SCT expression as the "q1" name. This is neither a local binding nor a fresh binding, and so no constraints are placed on the dependency. Note that without coindexing the long distance dependency would continue to hold, only under the "q" name.

```
val ex22 =
( fn fh =>
  ( fn lc =>
    ( ( pro ["personalc"] fh ["entity"] ( "ENTITY",
          "personalentity") "you")
      "arg0"
      ( md fh "can" free
        ( embVerb lc "event" ["arg0"] "judge"
          ( that lc
            ( question fh
              ( ( some lc fh "qentity"
                  ( nn lc ""))
                "q1"
                ( ( arg "q1")
                  "arg0"
                  ( verb lc "event" ["arg0"] "works"))))))))))
  ["arg0", "that", "arg1", "h"])
["ENTITY", "qentity", "event"]
```

The following demonstrates evaluation of ex22:

```
> SctToLang.eval (
    fn _ => nil,
```

```
    closureEnv "∃" ("ENTITY", "entity")
      ["ENTITY", "qentity", "event"] ex22);
```
val it =
Quant ("ENTITY", ["event", "ENTITY"], "∃", [],
 Quant ("event", ["event", "ENTITY"], "∃", [X (1, "event")],
  QuantThrow ("ENTITY", X (2, "personalentity"),
   REL ("", [Throw ("ENTITY", REL ("you:pick", [X (2, "personalentity")])]),
   REL ("can", [
    REL ("judge", [At (X (2, "personalentity"), "arg0"),
    At (X (1, "event"), "event"),
    At (
     REL ("QUEST", [
      Quant ("qentity", ["qentity"], "?", [X (3, "entity")],
       Quant ("event", ["event"], "∃", [X (4, "event")],
        REL ("", [Throw ("qentity", REL ("", [At (X (3, "entity"), "h")])]),
        REL ("works", [At (X (3, "entity"), "arg0"),
         At (X (4, "event"), "event")])])))]), "that")])])])))
: Lang.t

With post-processing and pretty printing the evaluation result produces:

$$\exists z_2 e_1 (z_2 = \text{you} \wedge \text{can}(\text{judge}(e_1, z_2, \text{QUEST}(?x_3 \exists e_4 \text{works}(e_4, x_3)))))$$

This shows the wh-dependency captured with the '?' closure from `question` and binding the main predicate *works* of the embedding as `"arg0"`. Also the event binding of *works* scopes with the embedding because of the `basic` existential closure of `question`.

As an example of a direct question, consider:

(15)   Who did Kim assure her that I would ask about her brother?

Example (15) is annotated:

```
(CP-QUE (WNP (WPRO Who))
        (IP-SUB (DOD did)
                (NP-SBJ (NPR Kim))
                (VB assure)
                (NP-OB1 (PRO her))
                (CP-THT (C that)
                        (IP-SUB (NP-OB1 *T*)
                                (NP-SBJ (PRO I))
                                (MD would)
                                (VB ask)
                                (PP (P about)
                                    (NP (PRO$ her)
                                        (N brother))))))
        (. ?))
```

Conversion arrives at ex23:

```
val ex23 =
( fn fh =>
  ( fn lc =>
    ( question fh
      ( ( some lc fh "qentity"
          ( nn lc ""))
        "q"
        ( ( npr "entity" "kim")
          "arg0"
          ( ( pro ["c"] fh ["entity"] ( "entity", "entity")
              "her")
            "arg1"
            ( embVerb lc "event" ["arg0", "arg1"] "did_assure"
              ( that lc
                ( ( pro ["personalc"] fh ["entity"]
                    ( "ENTITY", "personalentity") "i")
                  "arg0"
                  ( md fh "would" free
                    ( ( arg "q")
                      "arg1"
                      ( ( some lc fh "entity"
                          ( ( pro ["c"] fh ["entity"]
                              ( "entity", "entity") "her")
                            "of"
                            ( nn lc "brother")))
                        "about"
                        ( verb lc "event" ["arg0", "arg1"]
                          "ask")))))))))))
  ["of", "about", "arg1", "arg0", "that", "h"])
["qentity", "constant", "entity", "ENTITY", "event"]
```

The following demonstrates evaluation of ex23:

```
> SctToLang.eval (
    fn _ => nil,
    Sct.CClose ("constant",
      closureEnv "∃" ("ENTITY", "entity")
        ["qentity", "entity", "ENTITY", "event"] ex23));
val it =
Quant ("ENTITY", ["event", "entity", "ENTITY"], "∃", [],
Quant ("entity", ["event", "entity", "ENTITY"], "∃", [],
 Quant ("event", ["event", "entity", "ENTITY"], "∃", [],
  REL ("QUEST", [
  Quant ("qentity", ["qentity"], "?", [X (1, "entity")],
```

Quant ("entity", ["event", "entity"], "∃", [X (2, "entity")],
Quant ("event", ["event", "entity"], "∃", [X (4, "event"), X (3, "event")],
REL ("", [Throw ("qentity", REL ("", [At (X (1, "entity"), "h")])),
QuantThrow ("entity", X (5, "entity"),
REL ("", [Throw ("entity", REL ("her:pick", [X (5, "entity")])),
REL ("did_assure", [At (C ("kim", "entity"), "arg0"),
At (X (5, "entity"), "arg1"), At (X (4, "event"), "event"),
At (
QuantThrow ("ENTITY", X (6, "personalentity"),
REL ("", [
Throw ("ENTITY", REL ("i:pick", [X (6, "personalentity")])),
REL ("would", [
REL ("", [
Throw ("entity",
QuantThrow ("entity", X (7, "entity"),
REL ("", [
Throw ("entity",
REL ("her:pick", [X (7, "entity"), X (1, "entity"),
C ("kim", "entity"), X (5, "entity")])),
REL ("brother", [At (X (2, "entity"), "h"),
At (X (7, "entity"), "of")])])))),
REL ("ask", [At (X (6, "personalentity"), "arg0"),
At (X (1, "entity"), "arg1"), At (X (2, "entity"), "about"),
At (X (3, "event"), "event")])])])])), "that")])])))])))])))

: Lang.t

With post-processing and pretty printing the evaluation result produces:

$\exists z_6 (z_6 = i \land$
$\quad \text{QUEST} (?x_1 \exists x_7 x_5 x_2 e_3 e_4 (x_5 = \text{her} \land x_7 = \text{her}\{x_1, \text{kim}, x_5\} \land$
$\qquad \text{is\_brother\_of}(x_2, x_7) \land$
$\qquad \text{did\_assure}(e_4, \text{kim}, x_5,$
$\qquad \text{would}(\text{ask}(e_3, z_6, x_1) \land \text{about}(e_3) = x_2)))))$

This shows how it is only following integration with arg of the unbounded dependency as a local binding that anaphoric pick up is possible. Thus x_5, created with the object pronoun *her* of the matrix clause, must depend on an antecedent from the external discourse context, while for x_7, created with the possessive pronoun *her* of the embedded clause, there is choice of linking with x_1 (the unbounded dependency), as well as *kim* or x_5. This illustrates the *crossover* phenomenon (Postal 1971) whereby an unbounded dependency is unavailable for serving as a pronominal antecedent until after fulfilling its argument binding role. Following placement of arg the unbounded dependency is first a local binding accessible to reciprocals. And with sufficient embedding the dependency is a binding of the discourse context, as happens with possessive pronoun *her* being inside a noun phrase restriction (see Sect. 3.3.7).

4.13 Relative Clauses (CP-REL)

Relative clauses are clauses that are syntactically embedded within a noun phrase and which function to restrict the reference of the noun phrase (Keenan and Comrie 1977). relc creates an embedded environment where all assigned sequence values to the names of lc (the local bindings) shift to the "c" name with subord, with the exception of the "h" (relative clause head) binding. Additionally the head binding shifts to become an x binding, and there is also a decrement with Sct.There of x support to remove the countable contribution of a wh-element primed to take an x binding internal to the relative clause, which is consequently set to receive the head binding.

```
val relc =
fn lc => fn x => fn e =>
 subord lc ["h"] (Sct.Lam ("h", x, Sct.There (x, e)))
```

Inclusion of non-restrictive relative clause content will be achieved with npExtra. The non-restrictive content is placed into the nuclear scope of the containing NP, that is, outside the restriction but under the scope of the containing NP. Yet when the containing NP is indefinite or definite, following post-processing, the non-restrictive material will scope with the restriction material of the containing NP because of Sct.Throw.

```
val npExtra =
fn lc => fn fh => fn v => fn e1 => fn e2 => fn x => fn e3 =>
 e2 x (manage fh [Sct.Throw (v, NP nil lc e1 x), e3])
```

With the annotation system, relative clauses have the same internal structure as indirect questions (see Sect. 4.12), having both a wh-position and a complementiser position always shown, whether filled or empty.

```
        (CP-REL (WNP (WPRO who))
                (C 0)
                (IP-SUB ...))

        (CP-REL (WNP 0)
                (C that)
                (IP-SUB ...))

        (CP-REL (WNP 0)
                (C 0)
                (IP-SUB ...))
```

For example, consider (16) from Clark (1866).

(16) But they, that fight for freedom, undertake the noblest cause mankind can have at stake.

Example (16) is annotated:

```
(IP-MAT (CONJ But)
        (NP-SBJ (PRO they)
                (, ,)
                (CP-REL (WNP 0)
                        (C that)
                        (IP-SUB (NP-SBJ *T*)
                                (VBP fight)
                                (PP (P for)
                                    (NP (N freedom))))))
        (, ,)
        (VBP undertake)
        (NP-OB1 (D the)
                (ADJS noblest)
                (N cause)
                (CP-REL (WNP 0)
                        (C 0)
                        (IP-SUB (NP-OB1 *T*)
                                (NP-SBJ (N+N mankind))
                                (MD can)
                                (HV have)
                                (PP (P at)
                                    (NP (N stake))))))
        (. .))
```

Conversion arrives at ex24. A non-restrictive relative clause encoding with npExtra
is triggered for the matrix subject, with the pronoun head *they* linking to an established
antecedent. By contrast, the matrix object is a restrictive relative clause. With both
types of relative clause the CP-REL tag transforms as relc. Moreover, there is annotation to mark a wh-pronoun, that, with conversion, yields some lc fh "qentity"
(nn lc ""). This opens a long distance dependency with the "q" name, which is
integrated as a local binding with arg as the conversion of the corresponding trace.
The contribution of arg is informed by the functional information that accompanies
the NP tag of the trace, so that with NP-SBJ the long distance dependency becomes
an "arg0" binding; and with NP-OB1, an "arg1" binding.

```
val ex24 =
( fn fh =>
  ( fn lc =>
    ( ( npExtra lc fh "group"
        ( relc lc "qgroup"
          ( ( some lc fh "qgroup"
              ( nn lc ""))
            "q"
            ( ( arg "q")
```

```
                        "arg0"
                    ( ( some lc fh "entity"
                        ( nn lc "freedom"))
                      "for"
                      ( verb lc "event" ["arg0"] "fight")))))
            ( pro ["c"] fh ["group"] ( "group", "group") "they"))
          "arg0"
        ( ( some lc fh "ENTITY"
            ( ( coord fh "∧"
                ( relc lc "qentity"
                  ( ( some lc fh "qentity"
                      ( nn lc ""))
                    "q"
                    ( ( some lc fh "ENTITY"
                        ( nn lc "mankind"))
                      "arg0"
                      ( md fh "can" exist
                        ( ( arg "q")
                          "arg1"
                          ( ( some lc fh "entity"
                              ( nn lc "stake"))
                            "at"
                            ( verb lc "event"
                              ["arg0", "arg1"] "have")))))))))
              ( ( coord fh "∧"
                  ( subord lc ["h"]
                    ( adj lc "noblest")))
                ( nn lc "cause"))))
            "arg1"
            ( verb lc "event" ["arg0", "arg1"] "undertake"))))
  ["at", "arg1", "arg0", "for", "h"])
["qentity", "qgroup", "entity", "event", "group", "ENTITY"]
```

The following demonstrates evaluation of ex24:

```
> SctToLang.eval (
    fn _ => nil,
    closureEnv "∃" ("ENTITY", "entity")
      ["qentity", "qgroup", "entity", "event", "group", "ENTITY"]
      ex24);
```

val it =
Quant ("ENTITY", ["event", "group", "entity", "ENTITY"], "∃", [X (2, "entity"), X
(1, "entity")],
  Quant ("entity", ["event", "group", "entity", "ENTITY"], "∃", [X (3, "entity")],
    Quant ("group", ["event", "group", "entity", "ENTITY"], "∃", [],
      Quant ("event", ["event", "group", "entity", "ENTITY"], "∃", [X (5, "event"), X (4,

"event")],

   QuantThrow ("group", X (6, "group"),

    REL ("", [Throw ("group", REL ("they:pick", [X (6, "group")]))),

    REL ("", [

     Throw ("group",

     REL ("", [Throw ("qgroup", REL ("", [At (X (6, "group"), "h")]))),

     REL ("", [Throw ("entity", REL ("freedom", [At (X (3, "entity"), "h")]))),

     REL ("fight", [At (X (6, "group"), "arg0"),

     At (X (3, "entity"), "for"), At (X (4, "event"), "event")])])])),

    REL ("", [

     Throw ("ENTITY",

     REL ("∧", [

     REL ("", [Throw ("qentity", REL ("", [At (X (2, "entity"), "h")]))),

     REL ("", [

      Throw ("ENTITY", REL ("mankind", [At (X (1, "entity"), "h")]))),

      REL ("can", [

       Quant ("entity", ["event", "group", "entity"], "∃", [X (7, "entity")],

       Quant ("group", ["event", "group", "entity"], "∃", [],

       Quant ("event", ["event", "group", "entity"], "∃", [X (8, "event")],

       REL ("", [

        Throw ("entity", REL ("stake", [At (X (7, "entity"), "h")]))),

        REL ("have", [At (X (1, "entity"), "arg0"),

        At (X (2, "entity"), "arg1"), At (X (7, "entity"), "at"),

        At (X (8, "event"), "event")])])))))])])],

     REL ("∧", [REL ("noblest", [At (X (2, "entity"), "h")]),

     REL ("cause", [At (X (2, "entity"), "h")])])])),

    REL ("undertake", [At (X (6, "group"), "arg0"),

    At (X (2, "entity"), "arg1"), At (X (5, "event"), "event")])])])])))))))

: Lang.t

With post-processing and pretty printing the evaluation result produces:

$\exists x_1 x_2 x_3 X_6 e_4 e_5 \, (X_6 = \text{they} \wedge \text{fight}(e_4, X_6) \wedge \text{for}(e_4) = x_3 \wedge$
$\text{freedom}(x_3) \wedge \text{mankind}(x_1) \wedge$
$\text{can}\,(\exists x_7 e_8 \, (\text{stake}(x_7) \wedge \text{have}(e_8, x_1, x_2) \wedge \text{at}(e_8) = x_7)) \wedge$
$\text{noblest}(x_2) \wedge \text{cause}(x_2) \wedge \text{undertake}(e_5, X_6, x_2))$

Relative clause content is seen integrated into the overall expression with coordination.

4.14 Free Relative Clauses (CP-FRL)

Free relatives have the same internal structure as indirect questions and relative clauses (see Sects. 4.12 and 4.13). However free relatives have no external head. With the annotation system the function of a free relative in the clause is indicated by enclosing the free relative within an otherwise empty set of appropriately labelled parentheses. For example, consider:

(17)   Do what you can!

Annotation of (17) places the free relative clause inside parentheses labelled NP-OB1:

```
(IP-IMP (DOI Do)
        (NP-OB1 (CP-FRL (WNP (WPRO what))
                        (C 0)
                        (IP-SUB (NP-OB1 *T*)
                                (NP-SBJ (PRO you))
                                (MD can))))
        (. !))
```

Conversion arrives at ex25. With dt (see Sect. 3.3.7), a fresh "qentity" binding will be created with 'EXH' quantification that shifts to an "h" binding inside the restriction and to an "arg1" binding outside. Note that the main predicate of the free-relative is elided or missing, and conversion reflects this absence with "xxx" as the main predicate.

```
val ex25 =
( fn fh =>
  ( fn lc =>
    ( ( dt lc fh "EXH" ( "qentity", "entity")
        ( relc lc "qentity"
          ( ( some lc fh "qentity"
              ( nn lc ""))
            "q"
            ( ( pro ["personalc"] fh ["entity"]
                ( "ENTITY", "personalentity") "you")
              "arg0"
              ( md fh "can" exist
                ( ( arg "q")
                  "arg1"
                  ( verb lc "event" ["arg0", "arg1"] "xxx")))))))
        "arg1"
        ( verb lc "event" ["arg1"] "do")))
  ["arg1", "arg0", "h"])
["qentity", "ENTITY", "event", "entity"]
```

The following demonstrates evaluation of ex25:

```
> SctToLang.eval (
    fn _ => nil,
    closureEnv "∃" ("ENTITY", "entity")
    ["qentity", "ENTITY", "event", "entity"] ex25);
```

val it =
Quant ("ENTITY", ["event", "entity", "ENTITY"], "∃", [],
Quant ("entity", ["event", "entity", "ENTITY"], "∃", [],
 Quant ("event", ["event", "entity", "ENTITY"], "∃", [X (1, "event")],
  Quant ("qentity", ["qentity"], "EXH", [X (2, "entity")],
   REL ("", [
    Throw ("qentity",
    REL ("", [Throw ("qentity", REL ("", [At (X (2, "entity"), "h")])),
    QuantThrow ("ENTITY", X (3, "personalentity"),
     REL ("", [
      Throw ("ENTITY", REL ("you:pick", [X (3, "personalentity")]))),
     REL ("can", [
       Quant ("entity", ["event", "entity"], "∃", [],
        Quant ("event", ["event", "entity"], "∃", [X (4, "event")],
        REL ("xxx", [At (X (3, "personalentity"), "arg0"),
        At (X (2, "entity"), "arg1"),
        At (X (4, "event"), "event")])))])))])]))),
    Quant ("qentity", ["qentity"], "∃", [],
    REL ("do", [At (X (2, "entity"), "arg1"),
    At (X (1, "event"), "event")]))])))))))
: Lang.t

With post-processing and pretty printing the evaluation result produces:

$\exists z_3 e_1 (z_3 = \text{you} \wedge \text{EXH} x_2 (\text{can} (\exists e_4 \text{xxx} (e_4, z_3, x_2)), \text{do} (e_1, \_, x_2)))$

This says to do the exhaustive value of what can be *xxx*-ed by the referent of *you*.
See Zeevat (2007) for details of a model theoretic realisation of the *EXH* operation.

4.15 Comparative Clauses (CP-CMP)

The annotation system structures comparatives as follows. The whole comparison is
treated as a single constituent labelled according to the category of the head. Thus, *as
old as* ... is labelled ADJP, *more cake than* ... is labelled NP, etc. The *as* or *than* introducing the comparative clause is labelled P and takes a CP-CMP complement. The PP
consisting of *as/than* and its clausal complement is treated as a daughter of the entire
comparison structure (not necessarily as a sister of the licensing comparative head).
The CP-CMP has the same internal structure as indirect questions, relatives and free
relatives (see Sects. 4.12, 4.13 and 4.14): a wh-operator (always empty) is coindexed
with a trace indicating the elided target of comparison. For example, consider:

(18)   Mary laughed as soon as she got

Example (18) is annotated:

```
(IP-MAT (NP-SBJ (NPR Mary))
        (VBD laughed)
        (ADVP (ADVR as)
              (ADV soon)
              (PP (P as)
                  (CP-CMP (WADVP-1 0)
                          (C 0)
                          (IP-SUB (ADVP-TMP *T*-1)
                                  (NP-SBJ (PRO she))
                                  (VBD got))))))
```

Conversion arrives at ex26. Notably, there is dt (see Sect. 3.3.7) with 'EXH' quantification to make the target of comparison an exhaustive "as" binding that has the CP-CMP complement to form the restriction content.

```
val ex26 =
( fn fh =>
  ( fn lc =>
    ( ( npr "entity" "mary")
      "arg0"
      ( ( advp lc fh "event"
            ( ( dt lc fh "EXH" ( "qtime", "time")
                ( relc lc "qtime"
                    ( ( some lc fh "qtime"
                        ( nn lc ""))
                      "q1"
                      ( ( pro ["c"] fh ["entity"] ( "entity",
                            "entity") "she")
                        "arg0"
                        ( ( arg "q1")
                          "tmp"
                          ( verb lc "event" ["arg0", "tmp"]
                            "got"))))))
              "as"
              ( adv lc "as_soon")))
          ( verb lc "event" ["arg0"] "laughed"))))
    ["tmp", "arg0", "as", "fact", "arg1", "h"])
["constant", "qtime", "entity", "event", "time"]
```

The following demonstrates evaluation of ex26:

```
> SctToLang.eval (
    fn _ => nil,
    Sct.CClose ("constant",
      closureEnv "∃" ("ENTITY", "entity")
```

```
      ["qtime", "entity", "event", "time"] ex26));
```
val it =
Quant ("entity", ["event", "time", "entity"], "∃", [],
Quant ("time", ["event", "time", "entity"], "∃", [],
 Quant ("event", ["event", "time", "entity"], "∃", [X (2, "event"), X (1, "event")],
  QuantThrow ("event", X (3, "situation"),
   REL ("", [
    Throw ("event",
     Quant ("qtime", ["qtime"], "EXH", [X (4, "time")],
      REL ("", [
       Throw ("qtime",
        REL ("", [Throw ("qtime", REL ("", [At (X (4, "time"), "h")]))),
         QuantThrow ("entity", X (5, "entity"),
          REL ("", [
           Throw ("entity",
            REL ("she:pick", [X (5, "entity"), C ("mary", "entity")])),
            REL ("got", [At (X (5, "entity"), "arg0"), At (X (4, "time"), "tmp"),
             At (X (1, "event"), "event")])]))])))),
          Quant ("qtime", ["qtime"], "∃", [],
           REL ("as_soon", [At (X (4, "time"), "as"),
            At (X (3, "situation"), "fact")]))])))),
        REL ("fact", [At (X (3, "situation"), "fact"),
         At (
          REL ("laughed", [At (C ("mary", "entity"), "arg0"),
           At (X (2, "event"), "event")]), "that")])]))))))
: Lang.t

With post-processing and pretty printing the evaluation result produces:

$\exists x_5 s_3 e_1 e_2 (\text{EXH}t_4 (\text{got}(e_1, x_5) \land \text{tmp}(e_1) = t_4, \text{is\_as\_soon\_as}(s_3, t_4)) \land$
$x_5 = \text{she}\{\text{mary}\} \land \text{is\_fact\_that}(s_3, \text{laughed}(e_2, \text{mary})))$

The comparison is integrated following the 'fact' analysis of Moore (1995) used for the analysis of adverbs in Sect. 4.8.

4.16 Tough Movement Complements (CP-TMC)

With the annotation system, tough movement complements of adjectives (e.g., *to please* in *easy to please*; Chomsky 1977) have the same structure as infinitival relatives, illustrated here with annotation of (19):

(19) Mary is easy to please.

```
(IP-MAT (NP-SBJ (NPR Mary))
        (BEP is)
```

```
         (ADJP (ADJ easy)
               (CP-TMC (WNP 0)
                       (IP-INF (NP-OB1 *T*)
                               (TO to)
                               (VB please))))
         (. .))
```

Conversion arrives at ex27, an analysis that removes "h" as a possible bound argument name for the adjective and gives the complement the form of a relative clause.

```
val ex27 =
( fn fh =>
  ( fn lc =>
    ( ( npr "entity" "mary")
      "arg0"
      ( ( someClassic lc fh ( "attrib", "attrib") nil
          ( embAdj (diff (lc, ["h"])) "easy"
            ( relc lc "qentity"
              ( ( some lc fh "qentity"
                  ( nn lc ""))
                "q"
                ( ( arg "q")
                  "arg1"
                  ( verb lc "event" ["arg1"] "please"))))))
        "attribute"
        ( verb lc "event" ["arg0", "attribute"] "is"))))
  ["that", "arg1", "attribute", "arg0", "h"])
["constant", "qentity", "event", "attrib"]
```

The following demonstrates evaluation of ex27:

```
> SctToLang.eval (
    fn _ => nil,
    Sct.CClose ("constant",
      closureEnv "∃" ("ENTITY", "entity")
      ["qentity", "event", "attrib"] ex27));
```

val it =
Quant ("attrib", ["event", "attrib"], "∃", [],
Quant ("event", ["event", "attrib"], "∃", [X (2, "event"), X (1, "event")],
 QuantThrow ("attrib", X (3, "attrib"),
  REL ("", [
  Throw ("attrib",
   REL ("easy", [
   REL ("", [Throw ("qentity", REL ("", [At (X (3, "attrib"), "h")])),
    REL ("please", [At (X (3, "attrib"), "arg1"),
     At (X (1, "event"), "event")])])])),
   REL ("is", [At (C ("mary", "entity"), "arg0"),

At (X (3, "attrib"), "attribute"), At (X (2, "event"), "event")])])))))
: Lang.t

With post-processing and pretty printing the evaluation result produces:

$\exists A_3 e_1 e_2 \, (\text{easy}\,(\text{please}\,(e_1, \; \_, \; A_3)) \; \wedge \; \text{is}\,(e_2, \; \text{mary}, \; A_3))$

Notably, while the relation between the attribute binding of the matrix clause and the object of the infinitive is not indicated with the annotation of (19), following evaluation the `"attribute"` binding of the matrix is found to serve as the `"arg1"` binding of the infinitive.

4.17 Clause-Adjoined Relative Clauses (CP-CAR)

Clause-adjoined relatives are continuative relatives which refer back to the whole sentence.

(20) The lamps are not lighted, which vexes me.

Occurring at the clause level, a clause-adjoined relative is annotated with CP-CAR functional information:

```
(IP-MAT (NP-SBJ (D The)
                (NS lamps))
        (BEP are)
        (NEG-LOW not)
        (VBN lighted)
        (, ,)
        (CP-CAR (WNP (WPRO which))
                (C 0)
                (IP-SUB (NP-SBJ *T*)
                        (VBP vexes)
                        (NP-OB1 (PRO me))))
        (. .))
```

Conversion arrives at `ex28`. The CP-CAR functional information introduces the standard `relc` operation of a relative clause, but additionally `advp` (see Sect. 4.8) and `Sct.Lam ("fact", "h", _)` integrate the relative clause content with the containing clause.

```
val ex28 =
( fn fh =>
  ( fn lc =>
    ( ( some lc fh "GROUP"
        ( nn lc "lamps"))
      "arg0"
      ( ( advp lc fh "event"
```

```
                    ( Sct.Lam ( "fact", "h",
                        relc lc "qsituation"
                        ( ( some lc fh "qsituation"
                            ( nn lc ""))
                          "q"
                          ( ( arg "q")
                            "arg0"
                            ( ( pro ["personalc"] fh ["entity"]
                                ( "ENTITY", "personalentity") "me")
                              "arg1"
                              ( verb lc "event" ["arg0", "arg1"]
                                "vexes")))))))
            ( neg fh exist
              ( verb lc "event" ["arg0"] "are_lighted")))))
    ["arg1", "arg0", "h"])
["GROUP", "qsituation", "ENTITY", "event"]
```

The following demonstrates evaluation of ex28:

```
> SctToLang.eval (
    fn _ => nil,
    closureEnv "∃" ("ENTITY", "entity")
      ["qsituation", "ENTITY", "event", "GROUP"] ex28);
val it =
```

Quant ("ENTITY", ["event", "GROUP", "ENTITY"], "∃", [],
Quant ("GROUP", ["event", "GROUP", "ENTITY"], "∃", [X (1, "group")],
Quant ("event", ["event", "GROUP", "ENTITY"], "∃", [X (2, "event")],
REL ("", [Throw ("GROUP", REL ("lamps", [At (X (1, "group"), "h")])),
QuantThrow ("event", X (3, "situation"),
REL ("", [
Throw ("event",
REL ("", [Throw ("qsituation", REL ("", [At (X (3, "situation"), "h")])),
QuantThrow ("ENTITY", X (4, "personalentity"),
REL ("", [
Throw ("ENTITY", REL ("me:pick", [X (4, "personalentity")])),
REL ("vexes", [At (X (3, "situation"), "arg0"),
At (X (4, "personalentity"), "arg1"),
At (X (2, "event"), "event")])])))])),
REL ("fact", [At (X (3, "situation"), "fact"),
At (
REL ("¬", [
Quant ("event", ["event"], "∃", [X (5, "event")],
REL ("are_lighted", [At (X (1, "group"), "arg0"),
At (X (5, "event"), "event")])])]), "that")])])))])))
: Lang.t

With post-processing and pretty printing the evaluation result produces:

$$\exists z_4 X_1 s_3 e_2 (\text{vexes}(e_2, \ s_3, \ z_4) \ \wedge \ \text{lamps}(X_1) \ \wedge \ z_4 \ = \ \text{me} \ \wedge$$
$$\text{is\_fact\_that}(s_3, \ \neg \ \exists e_5 \text{are\_lighted}(e_5, \ X_1)))$$

This says a situation of the lamps not being lighted exists and this situation vexes the referent of *me*.

4.18 Phrasal Conjunction (CONJP)

Phrasal conjunction is brought about with operations sensitive to what is being conjoined. Specifically, distinct operations are required for conjoining lists of noun phrases, achieved below with either conjNpSum or conjNp, as opposed to preposition phrases to be conjoined with conjPp, and other phrase levels to be conjoined with conj.

```
val conjNpSum =
fn lc => fn fh => fn v => fn s => fn es => fn x => fn f =>
 let
  val conjunct =
  fn e =>
   exist fh (
    e "link" (rel "" [
     Sct.At (Sct.T ("link", 0), "h"),
     Sct.At (Sct.T ("h", 0), "of")]))
 in
  some lc fh v
   (Sct.Rel (fh, map (fn _ => "c") fh, s, map conjunct es)) x f
 end

val conjNp =
fn fh => fn s => fn env => fn es => fn x => fn f =>
 Sct.Rel
  (fh, map (fn _ => "c") fh, s, map (fn e => env fh (e x f)) es)

val conjPp =
fn fh => fn s => fn env => fn es => fn f =>
 Sct.Rel
  (fh, map (fn _ => "c") fh, s, map (fn e => env fh (e f)) es)

val conj =
fn fh => fn s => fn env => fn es =>
 Sct.Rel
  (fh, map (fn _ => "c") fh, s, map (fn e => env fh e) es)
```

conjNp, conjPp and conj have an env parameter to bring about closures, e.g., with exist, or not, with free (see Sect. 3.3.4). conjNpSum is defined with exist inbuilt.

For phrasal conjunction, the annotation system labels the second and following conjuncts as CONJPs, headed by a conjunction word if present, and adjoined to the first conjunct at the phrasal level. Cases can arise with no explicit conjunction at all, but absence of the CONJP head is most common when there are more than two conjuncts, with the conjunction appearing only before the final conjunct, as illustrated in the following schema:

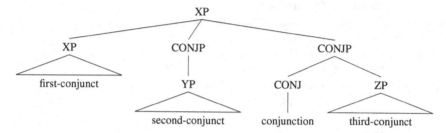

As an example with conjunction at both the noun phrase and verb phrase levels, consider:

(21)   Bell makes and distributes electronic, computer and building products.

Example (21) is annotated:

```
(IP-MAT (NP-SBJ (NPR Bell))
        (VP (VP (VBP makes))
            (CONJP (CONJ and)
                   (VP (VBP distributes))))
        (NP-OB1 (NP (ADJ electronic))
                (, ,)
                (CONJP (NP (N computer)))
                (CONJP (CONJ and)
                       (NP (ADJ building)
                           (NS products)
                           (COPY *))))
        (. .))
```

Conversion can arrive at the SCT expression ex29, with the contribution of the conjoined noun phrases integrated with conjNpSum and the contribution of the conjoined verb phrases integrated with conj. Also note inclusion of the tag COPY (with (COPY *)) in the annotation of (21). Prior to conversion, the content of the immediate left sister of an instance of COPY is copied to all other conjuncts of the conjunction.

```
val ex29 =
( fn fh =>
  ( fn lc =>
    ( ( npr "entity" "bell")
```

```
      "arg0"
      ( conjNpSum lc fh "group" "∧"
        [
          some lc fh "group"
            ( ( coord fh "∧"
                ( subord lc ["h"]
                  ( adj lc "electronic")))
              ( nn lc "products")),
          some lc fh "group"
            ( nn lc "computer_products"),
          some lc fh "group"
            ( ( coord fh "∧"
                ( subord lc ["h"]
                  ( adj lc "building")))
              ( nn lc "products"))
        ]
        "arg1"
        ( conj fh "∧" free
          [
            verb lc "event" ["arg0", "arg1"] "makes",
            verb lc "event" ["arg0", "arg1"] "distributes"
          ]))))
    ["arg1", "arg0", "h"])
["constant", "event", "group"]
```

The following demonstrates evaluation of ex29:

```
> SctToLang.eval (
    fn _ => nil,
    Sct.CClose ("constant",
      closureEnv "∃" ("ENTITY", "entity")
        ["event", "group"] ex29));
```

val it =
Quant ("group", ["event", "group"], "∃", [X (1, "group")],
 Quant ("event", ["event", "group"], "∃", [X (3, "event"), X (2, "event")],
  REL ("", [
   Throw ("group",
    REL ("∧", [
     Quant ("group", ["event", "group"], "∃", [X (4, "group")],
     Quant ("event", ["event", "group"], "∃", [],
      REL ("", [
       Throw ("group",
        REL ("∧", [REL ("electronic", [At (X (4, "group"), "h")]),
         REL ("products", [At (X (4, "group"), "h")])])),
        REL ("", [At (X (4, "group"), "h"), At (X (1, "group"), "of")])]))),
      Quant ("group", ["event", "group"], "∃", [X (5, "group")],

Quant ("event", ["event", "group"], "∃", [],
 REL ("", [
  Throw ("group", REL ("computer_products", [At (X (5, "group"), "h")])),
  REL ("", [At (X (5, "group"), "h"), At (X (1, "group"), "of")])]))),
 Quant ("group", ["event", "group"], "∃", [X (6, "group")],
 Quant ("event", ["event", "group"], "∃", [],
  REL ("", [
  Throw ("group",
  REL ("∧", [REL ("building", [At (X (6, "group"), "h")]),
   REL ("products", [At (X (6, "group"), "h")])])),
  REL ("", [At (X (6, "group"), "h"), At (X (1, "group"), "of")])])))])))),
 REL ("∧", [
 REL ("makes", [At (C ("bell", "entity"), "arg0"),
 At (X (1, "group"), "arg1"), At (X (2, "event"), "event")]),
 REL ("distributes", [At (C ("bell", "entity"), "arg0"),
 At (X (1, "group"), "arg1"), At (X (3, "event"), "event")])])])))
: Lang.t

With post-processing and pretty printing the evaluation result produces:

$\exists X_1 e_2 e_3$ (
 $\exists X_4$ (electronic (X_4) ∧ products (X_4) ∧ $X_4 \subseteq X_1$) ∧
 $\exists X_5$ (computer_products (X_5) ∧ $X_5 \subseteq X_1$) ∧
 $\exists X_6$ (building (X_6) ∧ products (X_6) ∧ $X_6 \subseteq X_1$) ∧
 makes $(e_2,$ bell, $X_1)$ ∧ distributes $(e_3,$ bell, X_1))

With the verbs in separate conjuncts, each creates a predicate with a distinct event binding, while sharing the inheritance of all other bindings: specifically, `"arg0"` and `"arg1"`. Furthermore the `"arg1"` binding, X_1, is restricted to be a group value that contains the members of a group of *electronic products*, X_4, a group of *computer products*, X_5, and a group of *building products*, X_6.

Evaluation following substitution of `conjNpSum fh "group" "∧"` in `ex29` for `conjNp fh "∧" free` produces:

$\exists X_1 X_2 X_3 e_4 e_5 e_6 e_7 e_8 e_9$ (electronic (X_1) ∧ products (X_1) ∧
computer_products (X_2) ∧ building (X_3) ∧ products (X_3) ∧
makes $(e_4,$ bell, $X_1)$ ∧ distributes $(e_5,$ bell, $X_1)$ ∧
makes $(e_6,$ bell, $X_2)$ ∧ distributes $(e_7,$ bell, $X_2)$ ∧
makes $(e_8,$ bell, $X_3)$ ∧ distributes $(e_9,$ bell, X_3))

The conjoined noun phrases no longer bring about a single binding restricted by their conjoined content, but rather each introduces a distinct binding for a distinct instance of the verb phrase content.

As an example of preposition phrase coordination, consider:

(22) The fish was cooked either under a grill or on the barbecue.

Example (22) is annotated:

```
(IP-MAT (NP-SBJ (D The)
                (N fish))
        (BED was)
        (VAN cooked)
        (PP (CONJ either)
            (PP (P under)
                (NP (D a)
                    (N grill)))
            (CONJP (CONJ or)
                   (PP (P on)
                       (NP (D the)
                           (N barbecue)))))))
        (. .))
```

Conversion yields ex30. Notably "either_or" is the relation name taken by conjPp, and, to bring about existential closures, there is exist (from Sect. 3.3.4).

```
val ex30 =
( fn fh =>
  ( fn lc =>
    ( ( some lc fh "ENTITY"
        ( nn lc "fish"))
      "arg0"
      ( conjPp fh "either_or" exist
        [
          ( some lc fh "entity"
            ( nn lc "grill"))
          "under",
          ( some lc fh "ENTITY"
            ( nn lc "barbecue"))
          "on"
        ]
        ( passive
          ( verb lc "event" ["arg1"] "cooked")))))
  ["under", "on", "arg0", "arg1", "by", "h"])
["ENTITY", "entity", "event"]
```

The following demonstrates evaluation of ex30:

```
> SctToLang.eval (
  fn _ => nil,
  closureEnv "∃" ("ENTITY", "entity")
    ["ENTITY", "entity", "event"] ex30);
```

val it =
Quant("ENTITY", ["event", "entity", "ENTITY"], "∃", [X(2, "entity"), X(1, "entity")],

Quant ("entity", ["event", "entity", "ENTITY"], "∃", [],
 Quant ("event", ["event", "entity", "ENTITY"], "∃", [],
  REL ("", [Throw ("ENTITY", REL ("fish", [At (X (2, "entity"), "h")])),
  REL ("either_or", [
   Quant ("entity", ["event", "entity"], "∃", [X (3, "entity")],
    Quant ("event", ["event", "entity"], "∃", [X (4, "event")],
     REL ("", [Throw ("entity", REL ("grill", [At (X (3, "entity"), "h")])),
      REL ("cooked", [At (X (2, "entity"), "arg1"),
       At (X (3, "entity"), "under"), At (X (4, "event"), "event")])])]))),
   Quant ("entity", ["event", "entity"], "∃", [],
    Quant ("event", ["event", "entity"], "∃", [X (5, "event")],
     REL ("", [Throw ("ENTITY", REL ("barbecue", [At (X (1, "entity"), "h")])),
      REL ("cooked", [At (X (2, "entity"), "arg1"), At (X (1, "entity"), "on"),
       At (X (5, "event"), "event")])])]))])]))])]))))
: Lang.t

With post-processing and pretty printing the evaluation result produces:

$\exists x_1 x_2$ (fish (x_2) ∧ barbecue (x_1) ∧
 either_or $(\exists x_3 e_4$ (grill (x_3) ∧ cooked $(e_4, \_, x_2)$ ∧ under $(e_4) = x_3)$,
 $\exists e_5$ (cooked $(e_5, \_, x_2)$ ∧ on $(e_5) = x_1)))$

Here, distinct bindings are integrated with *on* and *under* into distinct instances of the clause material to which the preposition phrase conjunction is attached placed under existential closures and connected by the relation of the conjunction.

As a final example of phrasal conjunction, consider clausal conjunction with verb phrase ellipsis:

(23)   John left in his car, and so did Bill.

Example (23) is annotated:

```
(IP-MAT (IP-MAT (NP-SBJ (NPR John))
                (VBD left)
                (COPY *)
                (PP (P in)
                    (NP (PRO$ his)
                        (N car)))
                (COPY *))
        (, ,)
        (CONJP (CONJ and)
               (IP-MAT (ADVP (ADV so))
                       (DOD did)        .
                       (NP-SBJ (NPR Bill))))
        (. .))
```

Conversion following copying triggered by the instances of COPY yields ex31.

```
val ex31 =
( fn fh =>
  ( conj fh "∧" free
    [
      ( fn lc =>
        ( ( npr "entity" "john")
          "arg0"
          ( ( some lc fh "entity"
              ( ( ( pro ["c"] fh ["entity"] ( "entity",
                    "entity") "his")
                  "of")
                ( nn lc "car")))
            "in"
            ( verb lc "event" ["arg0", "in"] "left"))))
      ["of", "in", "arg0", "arg1", "h"],
      ( fn lc =>
        ( ( npr "entity" "bill")
          "arg0"
          ( ( advp lc fh "event"
              ( adv lc "so"))
            ( ( some lc fh "entity"
                ( ( ( pro ["c"] fh ["entity"] ( "entity",
                      "entity") "his")
                    "of")
                  ( nn lc "car")))
              "in"
              ( verb lc "event" ["arg0", "in"] "did_left")))))
      ["of", "in", "fact", "arg0", "arg1", "h"]
    ]))
["constant", "entity", "event"]
```

The following demonstrates evaluation of ex31:

```
> SctToLang.eval (
    fn _ => nil,
    Sct.CClose ("constant",
      closureEnv "∃" ("ENTITY", "entity")
      ["entity", "event"] ex31));
```

val it =
Quant ("entity", ["event", "entity"], "∃", [X (2, "entity"), X (1, "entity")],
Quant ("event", ["event", "entity"], "∃", [X (4, "event"), X (3, "event")],
  REL ("∧", [
  REL ("", [
  Throw ("entity",
  QuantThrow ("entity", X (5, "entity"),
  REL ("", [

Throw ("entity",
  REL ("his:pick", [X (5, "entity"), C ("john", "entity")])),
  REL ("car", [At (X (1, "entity"), "h"), At (X (5, "entity"), "of")])]))),
REL ("left", [At (C ("john", "entity"), "arg0"), At (X (1, "entity"), "in"),
  At (X (3, "event"), "event")])]),
REL ("", [Throw ("event", REL ("so", [At (X (4, "event"), "fact")])),
REL ("", [
  Throw ("entity",
  QuantThrow ("entity", X (6, "entity"),
   REL ("", [
    Throw ("entity",
    REL ("his:pick", [X (6, "entity"), C ("bill", "entity"),
     X (1, "entity"), C ("john", "entity")])),
     REL ("car", [At (X (2, "entity"), "h"), At (X (6, "entity"), "of")])]))),
     REL ("did_left", [At (C ("bill", "entity"), "arg0"),
     At (X (2, "entity"), "in"), At (X (4, "event"), "event")])])])])))
: Lang.t

With post-processing and pretty printing the evaluation result produces:

$\exists x_6 x_5 x_1 x_2 e_3 e_4 \, (\text{so}(e_4) \, \wedge \, x_5 \, = \, \text{his\{john\}} \, \wedge \, \text{is\_car\_of}(x_1, \, x_5) \, \wedge$
$x_6 \, = \, \text{his\{bill,} \, x_1, \, \text{john\}} \, \wedge \, \text{is\_car\_of}(x_2, \, x_6) \, \wedge$
$\text{left}(e_3, \, \text{john}) \, \wedge \, \text{in}(e_3) \, = \, x_1 \, \wedge \, \text{did\_left}(e_4, \, \text{bill}) \, \wedge \, \text{in}(e_4) \, = \, x_2)$

While x_5 has *john* as antecedent, for x_6 there are several potential antecedents, capturing the 'sloppy identity' / 'strict identity' contrast of Ross (1967). Resolving x_6 to *bill* derives the sloppy reading, in which Bill's leaving is in Bill's car. The strict reading, in which Bill's leaving is in John's car, follows from resolving x_6 to *john*.

4.19 Parentheticals

Inclusion into an SCT expression of NP parentheticals that occur with a placement internal to an NP restriction will be achieved with npParenthetical. Similarly PP parentheticals inside an NP restriction will be integrated with ppParenthetical.

```
val npParenthetical =
fn fh => fn v => fn s => fn e1 => fn e2 => fn x => fn e3 =>
 e2 x (manage fh [
  Sct.Throw (v, e1 "" (rel s [Sct.T (x, 0), Sct.T ("", 0)])),
  e3])
```

```
val ppParenthetical =
fn lc => fn fh => fn v => fn e1 => fn e2 => fn x => fn e3 =>
 e2 x (
  manage fh [Sct.Throw (v, NP nil lc (e1 (nn lc ""))) x), e3])
```

Similar to npExtra of Sect. 4.13, integration places the parenthetical material inside
the scope of the containing NP but outside the restriction, with Sct.Throw ensuring
the parenthetical material scopes with the restriction material of the containing NP
when indefinite or definite.

With the annotation system, the label -PRN is added to any constituent acting as
an appositive or parenthetical.

(24)   Alonzo (a cat) isn't chasing the dog (near Yasuko).

Example (24) is annotated as follows:

```
(IP-MAT (NP-SBJ (NPR Alonzo)
                (-LRB- -LRB-)
                (NP-PRN (D a)
                        (N cat))
                (-RRB- -RRB-))
        (BEP $is)
        (NEG $n't)
        (VAG chasing)
        (NP-OB1 (D the)
                (N dog)
                (-LRB- -LRB-)
                (PP-PRN (P near)
                        (NP (NPR Yasuko)))
                (-RRB- -RRB-))
        (. .))
```

Conversion arrives at 0ex32:

```
val ex32 =
( fn fh =>
  ( fn lc =>
    ( ( npParenthetical fh "entity" "="
        ( some lc fh "entity"
          ( nn lc "cat"))
        ( npr "entity" "alonzo"))
      "arg0"
      ( neg fh exist
        ( ( ppParenthetical lc fh "ENTITY"
            ( ( npr "entity" "yasuko")
              "near")
            ( some lc fh "ENTITY"
              ( nn lc "dog")))
          "arg1"
          ( verb lc "event" ["arg0", "arg1"] "is_chasing")))))
  ["near", "arg1", "arg0", "h"])
["entity", "constant", "ENTITY", "event"]
```

The following demonstrates evaluation of `ex32`:

```
> SctToLang.eval (
    fn _ => nil,
    Sct.CClose ("constant",
     closureEnv "∃" ("ENTITY", "entity")
      ["entity", "ENTITY", "event"] ex32));
```

val it =
Quant ("ENTITY", ["event", "entity", "ENTITY"], "∃", [X (1, "entity")],
  Quant ("entity", ["event", "entity", "ENTITY"], "∃", [X (2, "entity")],
   Quant ("event", ["event", "entity", "ENTITY"], "∃", [],
    REL ("", [
     Throw ("entity",
      REL ("", [Throw ("entity", REL ("cat", [At (X (2, "entity"), "h")])),
       REL ("=", [C ("alonzo", "entity"), X (2, "entity")])])]),
      REL ("¬", [
       Quant ("entity", ["event", "entity"], "∃", [],
        Quant ("event", ["event", "entity"], "∃", [X (3, "event")],
         REL ("", [Throw ("ENTITY", REL ("dog", [At (X (1, "entity"), "h")])),
          REL ("", [
           Throw ("ENTITY",
            REL ("", [At (X (1, "entity"), "h"),
             At (C ("yasuko", "entity"), "near")])),
            REL ("is_chasing", [At (C ("alonzo", "entity"), "arg0"),
             At (X (1, "entity"), "arg1"),
             At (X (3, "event"), "event")])])])))])])))])])))
: Lang.t

With post-processing and pretty printing the evaluation result produces:

$\exists x_1 x_2 (\text{cat}(x_2) \wedge \text{alonzo} = x_2 \wedge \text{dog}(x_1) \wedge \text{is\_near}(x_1, \text{yasuko}) \wedge$
$\neg \exists e_3 \text{is\_chasing}(e_3, \text{alonzo}, x_1))$

With post-processing the PP restriction stating that the dog is *near Yasuko* has placement outside the scope of negation at the `discourse` level of closure which captures *the dog*.

4.20 Speech Parentheticals (IP-MAT-PRN)

For speech parentheticals (HE SAID, QUOTH SHE, etc.) the definition of `emptyC` realises a mechanism for reallocating the content of the parenthetical and external context to `"personalc"` before entering the direct speech, which receives a discourse level existential closure. With the approach to pronouns in Sect. 3.3.6, sequence values assigned `"personalc"` are accessible antecedents for personal pronouns.

```
val emptyC =
fn fh => fn e =>
 Sct.Clean (0, ["c"], "personalc",
  closureEnv "∃" ("ENTITY", "entity") fh e)
```

As an example, consider:

(25) "Come on," Nasha said. "Up beside me."

Example (25) is annotated as follows:

```
(IP-IMP-SPE (" ")
            (VBI Come)
            (RP on)
            (, ,)
            (" ")
            (IP-MAT-PRN (NP-SBJ (NPR Nasha))
                        (VBD said)
                        (. .))
            (" ")
            (PP (P Up)
                (PP (P beside)
                    (NP (PRO me))))
            (. .)
            (" "))
```

Conversion arrives at ex33, with the content of the speech parenthetical receiving the content of the speech as its complement.

```
val ex33 =
( fn fh =>
  ( fn lc =>
    ( ( npr "entity" "nasha")
      "arg0"
      ( embVerb lc "event" ["arg0"] "said"
        ( that lc
          ( ( emptyC fh)
            ( ( pro ["personalc"] fh ["entity"]
                ( "ENTITY", "personalentity") "me")
              "up_beside"
              ( verb lc "event" nil "come_on"))))))))
  ["up_beside", "that", "arg0", "arg1", "h"])
["constant", "ENTITY", "event"]
```

The following demonstrates evaluation of ex33:

```
> SctToLang.eval (
    fn _ => nil,
    Sct.CClose ("constant",
```

```
        closureEnv "∃" ("ENTITY", "entity")
          ["ENTITY", "event"] ex33));
```

val it =
Quant ("ENTITY", ["event", "ENTITY"], "∃", [],
 Quant ("event", ["event", "ENTITY"], "∃", [X (1, "event")],
  REL ("said", [At (C ("nasha", "entity"), "arg0"), At (X (1, "event"), "event"),
  At (
   Quant ("ENTITY", ["event", "ENTITY"], "∃", [],
    Quant ("event", ["event", "ENTITY"], "∃", [X (2, "event")],
    QuantThrow ("ENTITY", X (3, "personalentity"),
     REL ("", [
     Throw ("ENTITY",
      REL ("me:pick", [X (3, "personalentity"), C ("nasha", "entity")])),
     REL ("come_on", [At (X (3, "personalentity"), "up_beside"),
     At (X (2, "event"), "event")])])))), "that")])))
: Lang.t

With post-processing and pretty printing the evaluation result produces:

$\exists e_1 \mathrm{said}(e_1, \mathrm{nasha},$
$\quad \exists z_3 e_2 (z_3 = \mathrm{me}\{\mathrm{nasha}\} \wedge \mathrm{come\_on}(e_2) \wedge \mathrm{up\_beside}(e_2) = z_3))$

Notably, *me* of the speech has *Nasha* of the speech parenthetical as an accessible antecedent.

4.21 Nouns of Address

The dash tag -VOC (vocative) marks nouns of address. As an example, consider:

(26)   It is your garden now, little children

Example (26) is annotated as follows:

```
(IP-MAT (NP-SBJ (PRO It))
        (BEP is)
        (NP-OB1 (NP-POS (BIND *GROUP*)
                        (PRO your))
                (N garden))
        (ADVP-TMP (ADV now))
        (, ,)
        (NP-VOC (ADJ little)
                (NS children))
        (. .))
```

Regardless of placement, with the scope hierarchy of Sect. 4.2 -VOC tagged elements scope highest within the clause. Conversion to an SCT expression is an opportunity to accordingly reorganise scope placement for conformance to the hierarchy:

```
val ex34 =
( fn fh =>
  ( fn lc =>
    ( ( some lc fh "GROUP"
        ( ( coord fh "∧"
            ( subord lc ["h"]
              ( adj lc "little")))
          ( nn lc "children")))
      "personalc"
      ( ( pro ["c"] fh ["entity"] ( "entity", "entity") "it")
        "arg0"
        ( ( some lc fh "entity"
            ( ( pro ["personalc"] fh ["group"]
                ( "GROUP", "personalgroup") "your")
              "of"
              ( nn lc "garden")))
          "arg1"
          ( ( advp lc fh "event"
              ( adv lc "now"))
            ( verb lc "event" ["arg0", "arg1"] "is")))))))
    ["fact", "of", "arg1", "arg0", "h"])
["entity", "GROUP", "event"]
```

In addition to high placement, -VOC has the consequence that any new binding
will be opened as a `"personalc"` binding, and so subsequently be available as a
potential antecedent for personal pronouns, while never being available to bind a
local argument.

The following demonstrates evaluation of ex34:

```
> SctToLang.eval (
    fn _ => nil,
    closureEnv "∃" ("ENTITY", "entity")
    ["entity", "GROUP", "event"] ex34);
```

val it =
Quant ("GROUP", ["event", "entity", "GROUP"], "∃", [X (1, "group")],
  Quant ("entity", ["event", "entity", "GROUP"], "∃", [X (2, "entity")],
    Quant ("event", ["event", "entity", "GROUP"], "∃", [X (3, "event")],
    REL ("", [
    Throw ("GROUP",
    REL ("∧", [REL ("little", [At (X (1, "group"), "h")]),
    REL ("children", [At (X (1, "group"), "h")])])),
    QuantThrow ("entity", X (4, "entity"),
    REL ("", [Throw ("entity", REL ("it:pick", [X (4, "entity")])]),
    REL ("", [
    Throw ("entity",
    QuantThrow ("GROUP", X (5, "personalgroup"),

REL ("", [
Throw ("GROUP",
REL ("your:pick", [X (5, "personalgroup"), X (1, "group")])),
REL ("garden", [At (X (2, "entity"), "h"),
At (X (5, "personalgroup"), "of")])]))),
REL ("", [Throw ("event", REL ("now", [At (X (3, "event"), "fact")])),
REL ("is", [At (X (4, "entity"), "arg0"), At (X (2, "entity"), "arg1"),
At (X (3, "event"), "event")])])])])))])))))
: Lang.t

With post-processing and pretty printing the evaluation result produces:

$\exists Z_5 X_1 x_4 x_2 e_3 (\text{now}(e_3) \wedge x_4 = \text{it} \wedge \text{is\_garden\_of}(x_2, Z_5) \wedge$
$\text{little}(X_1) \wedge \text{children}(X_1) \wedge Z_5 = \text{your}\{X_1\} \wedge \text{is}(e_3, x_4, x_2))$

Because of the approach to pronouns in Sect. 3.3.6, *your*, having as accessible bindings the values of the sequence assigned to `"personalc"`, has the contribution of *little children* as a possible antecedent. In contrast, *it* needs values to be of the sequence assigned to `"c"` in order to be possible antecedents.

4.22 Summary

To sum up, this chapter described treebank annotation for English sentences from which meaning representations were automatically derived following conversion to SCT expressions. Broad coverage was demonstrated with examples of passives, adverbial clauses, participial clauses, adjectives, adverbs, floating quantifiers, pronominal binding, covaluation arising because of embedding, wh-questions, relative clauses, free relative clauses, comparative clauses, tough movement complements, clause-adjoined relative clauses, phrasal conjunction, speech parentheticals and nouns of address.

Advantages of the adopted annotation scheme were highlighted. Most notably, clause level functional information was vital to determining either coordinating or subordinating structure for representations of meaning beyond the predicate-argument level. Having an internal syntax where phrasal categories are fundamentally similar greatly assisted generalising the approach. Having bracketed syntactic structure at the clause level inherently flat admitted a simple addition of scope information.

References

Aho A, Brian K, Peter W (1988) The Awk programming language. Addison-Wesley Publishing Company, Reading

Ann B, Ferguson M, Katz K, MacIntyre R (1995) Bracketing guidelines for Treebank II style Penn Treebank project. Technical Report MS-CIS-95-06, LINC LAB 281, University of Pennsylvania Computer and Information Science Department

Bouchard D (1985) PRO, pronominal or anaphor. Linguist. Inq. 16:471–477

Chomsky N (1977) On WH-movement. In: Culicover P, Wasow T, Akmajan A (eds) Formal syntax. Academic Press, New York, pp 71–132

Clark SW (1866) A practical grammar: in which words, phrases, and sentences are classified according to their offices; and their various relations to one another, illustrated by a complete system of diagrams. A. S. Barnes & Co, New York

Donald D (1967) The logical form of action sentences. In: Rescher N (ed) The logic of decision and action. University of Pittsburgh Press, Pittsburgh. Reprinted. In: Davidson D (1980) Essays on actions and events, pp. 105–122. Claredon Press, Oxford

Kamp H (1981) A theory of truth and semantic representation. In: Groenendijk J, Janssen T, Stokhof M (eds) Formal methods in the study of language. Mathematical Centre, Amsterdam, pp 277–322

Heim I (1993) Anaphora and semantic interpretation: a reinterpretation of Reinhart's approach. Technical Report SfS-Report-07-93, University of Tübingen

Huddleston R, Pullum Geoffrey K (2002) The Cambridge grammar of the English language. Cambridge University Press, Cambridge

Higginbotham J (1980) Pronouns and bound variables. Linguist Rev 11:679–708

Keenan E, Bernard C (1977) Noun phrase accessibility and universal grammar. Linguist. Inq. 8(1):63–99

Kroch A, Santorini B, Delfs L (2004) The Penn-Helsinki parsed corpus of early modern English (PPCEME). Department of Linguistics, University of Pennsylvania, CD-ROM, first edition

Kroch A, Santorini B, Diertani A (2010) The Penn-Helsinki parsed corpus of modern British English (PPCMBE). Department of Linguistics, University of Pennsylvania, CD-ROM, second edition

Moore RC (1995) Logic and representation. CSLI Publications, Stanford

Partee B (1975) Deletion and variable binding. In: Keenan E (ed) Formal semantics of natural language. Cambridge University Press, Cambridge, pp 16–34

Paul P (1971) Cross-over phenomena holt. Rinehart and Winston, New York

Payne ET (2010) Understanding English grammar: a linguistic introduction. Cambridge University Press, Cambridge

Ross JR (1967) Constraints on variables in syntax. Ph.D. thesis, MIT, Cambridge

Santorini B (2010) Annotation manual for the Penn Historical Corpora and the PCEEC (Release 2). Department of Computer and Information Science, University of Pennsylvania, Philadelphia, Technical report

Taylor A (1999) PPCME lite: a brief introduction to syntactic annotation system of the PPCME2. University of Pennsylvania, Technical report

Taylor A, Nurmi A, Warner A, Pintzuk S, Nevalainen T (2006) The York-Helsinki parsed corpus of early English correspondence (PCEEC). Department of Linguistics, University of York, Oxford Text Archive, first edition

Zeevat H (2007) Exhaustivity, questions and plurals in update semantics. In: Aloni M, Butler A, Dekker P (eds) Questions in dynamic semantics, pp. 161–192. Elsevier, Amsterdam

Appendix A
Standard ML Introduction

Standard ML implementations are predominately interactive, so participating in and observing program behaviour can be immediate. Start an interactive interpreter for Standard ML. Expressions or declarations are typed at the prompt. Expression evaluation occurs when a semicolon is typed followed by ENTER. If ENTER is pressed without a preceding semicolon, the interpreter continues to accept input, only from a new line. Here are examples, where human-typed things are in the `teletype` font, and responses of the machine are in *italic* font. The prompt is a greater than symbol '>'. The interpreter maintains a special expression `it` which always evaluates to the last successful result.

```
> 3 + 5;
```
val it = 8: int

```
> "un" ^ "lock" ^ "able";
```
val it = "unlockable": string

```
> print (it ^ "\n");
```
unlockable
val it = (): unit

```
> fn x => x + 1;
```
val it = fn: int -> int

Declarations can also be introduced as follows,

```
> val n = 1;
```
val n = 1: int

```
> val succ = fn x => x + 1;
```
val succ = fn: int -> int

© Springer International Publishing Switzerland 2015
A. Butler, *Linguistic Expressions and Semantic Processing*,
DOI 10.1007/978-3-319-18830-0

which binds n to 1 and succ to the successor function on integers that returns an expected number with 1 added. Thus:

```
> succ n;
val it = 2: int
```

Standard ML is strongly and statically typed. That is, each expression is assigned a type describing the values it can evaluate to. Although the language is statically typed, type annotations are rarely needed in the code, as most types can be inferred. For example, in typing val n = 1 above, nothing was said about n being an integer, but the response from Standard ML shows this was figured out.

Type checking ensures that only compatible operations are performed. This helps eliminate many mistakes during preliminary stages of code writing, and greatly facilitates tracking changes with revisions. For example, code that adds together a number and a string will fail, with the location of the problem pinpointed. Also having Standard ML determine the type of a function can be useful for understanding what the function says.

Standard ML provides common basic types such as booleans, integers, floating points, characters, and strings, as well as compound types such as tuples, records, lists, and arrays to create complex data objects, as well as the means to create novel types with datatypes.

For certain arguments functions can be undefined (as opposed to nonterminating), in which case an exception is raised that interrupts the current evaluation.

A.1 Let-Expressions

An expression with local declarations can be formed as follows:

```
> let
    val n = 1
    val succ = fn x => x + 1
  in
    succ n * succ n
  end;
val it = 4: int
```

A.2 If-Then-Else-Expressions

The syntax for if-then-else expressions is as follows,

```
if expression₀ then expression₁ else expression₂
```

where $expression_0$ needs to have the type bool and $expression_1$ and $expression_2$ must have the same type.

A.3 Case-Expressions

Another form of expression involves pattern matching,

```
case expression₀ of
   pattern₁ => expression₁
| ...
| patternₙ => expressionₙ
```

which evaluates $expression_0$ to a value v, chooses the first clause $pattern_i$ => $expression_i$ such that v matches $pattern_i$, and then evaluates $expression_i$ after introducing bindings for the variables in $pattern_i$. If v matches none of the patterns $pattern_1$, ..., $expression_n$, a Match exception is raised. For example, the above if-then-else expression is equivalent to the following case expression:

```
case expression₀ of
   true => expression₁
| false => expression₂
```

A.4 Type Variables

A name starting with a single quote, 'a, 'b and so on, stands for a type variable. A name starting with two single quotes, ''a, ''b and so on, stands for a type variable restricted to equality types.

A.5 Tuples

Tuples are formed by placing comma separated components inside round brackets. For a tuple of length n, there are n projections #1, ..., #n for selecting the components of the tuple. Here are some examples (note '<>' is the inequality operator of type ''a * ''a -> bool, which returns true when '=' would return false, and vice versa):

```
> val x = (2 + 2, 3 <> 4, #"a", "a");
val x = (4, true, #"a", "a"): int * bool * char * string

> #1 x;
val it = 4: int

> #2 x;
val it = true: bool

> #3 x;
val it = #"a": char

> #4 x;
val it = "a": string
```

A.6 Lists

Given a type `'a`, `'a list` is the type for lists in which each element is of type `'a`. The constructor `nil` represents the empty list, and the infix constructor `::` (with right associativity) takes an element and a list to form another list. For example, `1 :: 2 :: 3 :: nil` is a list of type `int list`. Alternatively, `[]` may be written for `nil` and `[1, 2, 3]` for `1 :: 2 :: 3 :: nil`. There are already various functions on lists that are built-in or available with the Basis library, notably:

- `null l` returns `true` if the list `l` is empty, and `false` otherwise.

- `hd l` returns the first element of `l`. An `Empty` exception is raised if `l` is `nil`.

- `tl l` returns all but the first element of `l`. An `Empty` exception is raised if `l` is `nil`.

- `List.last l` returns the last element of `l`. An `Empty` exception is raised if `l` is nil.

- `List.nth (l, i)` returns the i(th) element of the list `l`, counting from `0`. A `Subscript` exception is raised if $i < 0$ or $i \geq$ `length l`. Ignoring exceptions, `List.nth (l, 0) = hd l`.

- `List.take (l, i)` returns the first i elements of the list `l`. A `Subscript` exceptions is raised if $i < 0$ or $i >$ `length l`. It holds that `List.take (l, length l) = l`.

- `List.drop (l, i)` returns what is left after dropping the first i elements of the list `l`. A `Subscript` exception is raised if $i < 0$ or $i >$ `length l`. It holds that `List.take (l, i)` `@ List.drop (l, i) = l` when $0 \leq i \leq$ `length l`. Also, `List.drop (l, length l) = []`.

- `length l` returns the number of elements in the list `l`.

- `rev l` returns a list consisting of `l`'s elements in reverse order.

- `l1 @ l2` returns the list that is the concatenation of `l1` and `l2`.

- `List.concat l` returns the list that is the concatenation of all the lists in `l` in order. `List.concat [l1, l2, ..., ln] = l1 @ l2 @ ... @ ln`

- `map f l` applies `f` to each element of `l` from left to right, returning the list of results.

- `List.filter f l` applies `f` to each element `x` of `l`, from left to right, and returns the list of those `x` for which `f x` evaluated to `true`, in the same order as they occurred in the argument list.

- `foldr f init [x1, x2, ..., xn]` returns `f(x1, f(x2, ..., f(xn, init)...))` or `init` if the list is empty.

- `foldl f init [x1, x2, ..., xn]` returns `f(xn,...,f(x2, f(x1, init))...)` or `init` if the list is empty.

- `List.exists f l` applies `f` to each element `x` of the list `l`, from left to right, until `f x` evaluates to `true`; it returns `true` if such an `x` exists and `false` otherwise.

- `List.all f l` applies `f` to each element `x` of the list `l`, from left to right, until `f x` evaluates to `false`; it returns `false` if such an `x` exists and `true` otherwise.

- `List.tabulate (n, f)` returns a list of length n equal to `[f(0), f(1), ..., f(n-1)]`, created from left to right. A `Size` exception is raised if $n < 0$.

A.7 Functions

Functions can be introduced with value declarations, as with `succ` above, or with `fun` syntax which offers a way to attach type information for self documentation purposes:

```
fun member (x: ''a, ys: ''a list): bool =
  List.exists (fn y => x = y) ys

fun diff (xs: ''a list, ys: ''a list): ''a list =
  List.filter (fn x => not (member (x, ys))) xs

fun inter (xs: ''a list, ys: ''a list): ''a list =
  List.filter (fn x => member (x, ys)) xs
```

Functions can perform pattern matching on an argument:

```
fun uniq (l: ''a list): ''a list =
  case l of
    nil => nil
  | h::t => h::uniq (diff (t, [h]))
```

The form:

```
fun f (x: t1): t2 =
 case x of
    pattern₁ => expression₁
  | ...
  | patternₙ => expressionₙ
```

can be written directly as:

```
fun f pattern₁ = expression₁
   | ...
   | f patternₙ = expressionₙ
```

Thus, the function `uniq` can also be declared through the following syntax:

```
fun uniq nil = nil
  | uniq (h::t) = h::uniq (diff (t, [h]))
```

Note the function name has to appear at every case alternative. A disadvantage over the explicit `case` form is that there is no longer a simple way to attach type information. For this reason, presentation with explicit `case` expressions is favoured throughout this book, except for very simple functions.

The following example declares two mutually recursive functions:

```
fun even (n: int): bool =
 if n = 0 then true else odd (n-1)
and odd (n: int): bool =
 if n = 0 then false else even (n-1)
```

When defining a function, some help functions or auxiliary functions may be defined. The following declaration is such an example.

```
fun iterate f cnt init =
 let
  fun iter (0, v) = v
    | iter (n, v) = iter (n-1, f v)
 in
  if cnt < 0 then
   raise Subscript
  else
   iter (cnt, init)
 end
```

`iterate f cnt a` invokes the function `f` `cnt` times, starting with the value `a`, and using the result of one iteration as the argument in the next. A `Subscript` exception is raised if `cnt` is negative.

A.8 Datatypes

The characteristic property of a constructed value is that it contains the values out of which it is built. For example, tuple (3, 5) is a constructed value, evaluating to the pair *(3, 5)* which contains *3* and *5*; by contrast 3 + 5 evaluates to *8*, which is not a constructed value.

Novel ways of constructing values from existing values are introduced with datatypes. The declaration of a new datatype consists of

1. the keyword datatype;
2. a type name;
3. an "=" sign;
4. a list of one or more constructor expressions separated by bars.

A constructor expression consists of:

1. a constructor name, usually an identifier beginning with a capital;
2. (optionally) the keyword "of" followed by a type expression.

For example, binary trees with integer terminal nodes can be introduced as follows:

```
datatype IntTree =
   ILeaf of int
 | INode of IntTree * IntTree
```

This says that a value of type IntTree is either of the form ILeaf i where i needs to have the type int, or of the form INode (t_1, t_2) where t_1 and t_2 must have type IntTree.

Function addints computing the sum of all terminal nodes can be defined through the use of pattern matching as follows:

```
fun addints (t: IntTree): int =
 case t of
   ILeaf i => i
 | INode (t1, t2) => addints t1 + addints t2
```

For example,

```
> addints (INode (ILeaf 5, INode (ILeaf ~21, ILeaf 18)));
val it = 2: int
```

Note negative numbers are written as ~21, the - sign being reserved for the subtraction operation.

The following declaration introduces a datatype constructor btree that forms the type 'a btree when applied a type 'a.

```
datatype 'a btree =
   Leaf of 'a
 | Node of 'a btree * 'a btree
```

The following is now possible:

```
> Node (Leaf 5, Node (Leaf ~21, Leaf 18));
```
val it = Node (Leaf 5, Node (Leaf ~21, Leaf 18)): int btree

```
> Node (Leaf "un", Node (Leaf "lock", Leaf "able"));
```
val it = Node (Leaf "un", Node (Leaf "lock", Leaf "able")): string btree

A.9 References

The following declaration

```
val cnt = ref 0
```

allocates some memory to store the integer value 0 and then binds the memory location to cnt. Note that the expression ref 0 itself is not a value; the reference returned from evaluating the expression is a value, but such a value cannot be expressed explicitly in Standard ML.

After the declaration, the type of cnt is int ref. The binding of cnt cannot be changed but the value stored in the memory location to which cnt is bound can be updated. For example, the value is updated to 1 after the expression cnt := 1 is evaluated. In general, an expression of the form e1 := e2 evaluates e1 to a reference r and e2 to a value v, and then stores the value v in the memory location bound to the reference r.

The dereference operator is !. For example, !e evaluates e to a reference r and then returns the value stored in the memory location bound to r. Equality on references is the usual pointer equality. Also, ref may be used to form patterns, as in the following incrementing method:

```
fun inc ((r as ref n): int ref): unit = (r := n+1)
```

A.10 Structures

Structures are part of the module system of Standard ML. They provide a way to group declarations.

```
structure S = struct

  datatype 'a btree =
     Leaf of 'a
   | Node of 'a btree * 'a btree

  fun foldtree (f: ('a * 'a -> 'a), t: 'a btree): 'a =
   case t of
```

```
    Leaf x => x
  | Node (t1, t2) => f (foldtree (f, t1), foldtree (f, t2))
```

end

A component in S can be referred to by appending S. to the front of the name of the component. For example, S.Leaf and S.Node have the types `'a -> 'a S.btree` and `'a S.btree * 'a S.btree -> 'a S.btree`, respectively; while:

```
> S.foldtree (
    Int.max,
    S.Node (S.Leaf 5, S.Node (S.Leaf ~21, S.Leaf 18)));
val it = 18: int
```

```
> S.foldtree (
    op ^,
    S.Node (S.Leaf "un", S.Node (S.Leaf "lock", S.Leaf "able")));
val it = "unlockable": string
```

```
> S.foldtree (
    op ^,
    S.Node (S.Node (S.Leaf "un", S.Leaf "lock"), S.Leaf "able"));
val it = "unlockable": string
```

Index

<>, 163
@, 164
Assign.manage, 27
Assign.pop, 26
Assign.popLast, 26
Assign.push, 26
Assign.shiftLast, 27
Assign.t, 26
Basic.t, 2
Davidsonian.argnt, 21
Davidsonian.format, 21
Davidsonian.rmArg, 21
FolSatisfy.eval, 12
Lang.t, 16
List.all, 165
List.concat, 164
List.drop, 164
List.exists, 165
List.filter, 165
List.last, 164
List.nth, 164
List.tabulate, 165
List.take, 164
NP, 38, 61
NP2, 43
PP, 39
Post.transform, 18
PrettyFol.eval, 8
SOMEONE, 35
Sct.allocate, 47
Sct.collect, 47
Sct.count, 47
Sct.manage, 47
Sct.sumcount, 47
Sct.t, 45
SctToLang.cnt, 50

SctToLang.env, 51
SctToLang.eval, 51
Self.names, 29
Self.t, 28
SelfToLang.cnt, 29
SelfToLang.env, 29
SelfToLang.eval, 30
addArgs, 41, 58
adj, 113
adv, 118
advp, 118
allSubeprs, 3
arg, 97
basic, 62
classic, 57
clean, 57
closeAll, 62
closureEnv, 63
cond, 100
conj, 146
conjNp, 146
conjNpSum, 146
conjPp, 146
control, 78
coord, 99
diff, 165
discourse, 62
dt, 75
embAdj, 113
embAdv, 118
embNn, 82
embVerb, 76
emptyC, 156
every, 73
exist, 63
filter, 70
floatingQuantifier, 121

© Springer International Publishing Switzerland 2015
A. Butler, *Linguistic Expressions and Semantic Processing*,
DOI 10.1007/978-3-319-18830-0

focusParticle, 123
foldl, 165
foldr, 165
free, 64
hd, 164
inc, 168
inter, 165
isBound, 4
isFree, 4
isReused, 6
isSentence, 4
iterate, 166
length, 164
manage, 57
map, 165
md, 64
member, 165
neg, 64
nn, 59
noun, 42
noun1, 39
npExtra, 135
npParenthetical, 153
npr, 68

null, 164
passive, 96
ppParenthetical, 153
predicate, 42, 59
pro, 70
question, 130
questioned, 62
rel, 58
relc, 135
rev, 164
selectClosures, 63
some, 64
someClassic, 61
someFact, 100
subord, 75
that, 75
tl, 164
toComp, 78
uniq, 165
varConv, 6
verb, 42, 64
verb1, 35
word, 42
word1, 41

Printed in the United States
By Bookmasters